AMAZON SELLER CLASSROOM IN A BOOK METHODS OF PRODUCT RESEARCH

AMAZON SELLER CLASSROOM IN A BOOK METHODS OF PRODUCT RESEARCH

DREW BERRY

Legal Notice:

ISBN-13: 9798610075495

Disclaimer:

The information provided herein is stated to be truthful and consistent, in that any liability, in terms of inattention or otherwise, by any usage or abuse of policies, processes, or directions contained within is the solitary and utter responsibility of the recipient reader. Under no circumstances will any legal responsibility or blame be held against the publisher for any reparation, damages, or monetary loss due to the information herein, either directly or indirectly.

Please note that the content within this document is for educational and informational purposes only. Every attempt has been made to provide accurate, up to date, and reliable complete information. No warranties of any kind are expressed or implied. By reading this document, the reader agrees that under no circumstances is the author or publisher responsible for any losses, direct or indirect, which are incurred as a result of the information contained within this document, including, but not limited to; errors, omissions, or inaccuracies.

Special Thanks:

Special thanks to the developers at Amazon, Google, and Helium 10 for providing the necessary software.

This book is dedicated to my readers.
May you each find great success as an
Amazon Seller!

Table Of Contents

Amazon Sellers Classroom In A Group | FBA & FBM Mastery
www.facebook.com/groups/amzsellers/

Free Gift: The Verified Purchase Of "Amazon Seller Methods Of Product Research" Includes A One-On-One (5) Question Live Email Correspondence With The Author

Introduction:

A Brief Excerpt On Who I Am, How I Became An Amazon Seller, & The Reason You Can Trust My Expertise:

I attended Cabrillo College in Aptos, California, USA where I earned an Associate Degree with emphasis on Graphic Design, Photography, and Communication. Post-graduation from Cabrillo College, I studied Creative Advertising and Online Marketing at San Jose State University in San Jose, California, USA. Upon completion of San Jose State University, I chose to study jewelry manufacturing and learned the creative process the profession entails. I designed, hand crafted, marketed and sold my unique pieces at farmers markets, art festivals, music events, as well as online. This was a wonderful line of employment for me because I not only enjoyed the design aspects of the business, but I also attained a thorough comprehension of how to effectively create an e-commerce presence through utilization of Etsy, Facebook, and Pinterest. Furthermore, from my experience I acquired an extensive understanding of the numerous processes owning and operating a successful business entails. I learned how to efficiently build a recognizable company from scratch and create an identifiable profitably viable brand that retailed unique high-quality merchandise. Although this was a lucrative venture and a comprehensive learning experience for me, I had reached a pinnacle in regard to how much I could grow as a business owner. This was due to the fact that I was the sole manufacturer of my products and I was often required to travel in order to vend my pieces at various events throughout the year. These specific attributes were often undesirably time consuming and financially daunting. These duties combined with the daily operational business related tasks left me no time to expand my business to the creative and monetary extent that I was striving to flourish. Ultimately, I was not reaching my full potential as a business owner therefore I chose to study alternative modes of product manufacturing and different retail avenues. Since I was no longer interested in being the sole manufacturer of my merchandise for my new e-commerce business ventures I extensively researched online product sourcing. Through trial and error, I taught myself how to locate reputable suppliers online, effectively communicate with them, build trusting relationships with them, and work with them to have my branded merchandise manufactured to my exact specifications. Now that I had attained the products, I necessitated a populated marketplace to vend my merchandise. I had chosen early on that I was not interested in owning a brick and mortar store therefore I researched several different online retail platform options available for business owners. Through my investigation I identified that Amazon was a high-traffic profitable sales arena and the perfect fit for my professional needs. Before I could begin to sell on Amazon I needed to acquire the crucial necessary knowledge required to become a successful Amazon Seller and maintain a long-lasting presence on the Amazon Marketplace. I devoted countless hours to aggressively researching all aspects of selling on Amazon. I then took the wealth of information I attained through my studies and constructed a business model I could follow. Now that I had product suppliers and an online avenue to retail my goods I no longer had to spend my time personally manufacturing my merchandise and traveling to sell it. I could instead focus my energy on designing products, sourcing them from manufacturers, and listing them for sale on the Amazon Marketplace. Being an Amazon Seller allows me to remain creative as well as expand my business exponentially. Throughout the process of building an Amazon based e-commerce empire I have created various successfully thriving brands, developed a firm professional trusting relationship with several manufacturers, fashioned a steadily growing extensive customer following, and assembled numerous lucrative Amazon product listings.

What this book does not contain is a onetime winning lottery ticket, an instructional booklet to earning so called passive income, a claim to teach you how to easily obtain fame and fortune, or a slew of unreasonably high figures in regard to potential earnable income. It is a truthful, realistic, and forthright comprehension of what is required of you mentally, physically, and financially to be a successful Amazon Seller. Researching and locating lucrative merchandise to retail on the Amazon Marketplace requires extensive knowledge, hard work, planning, determination, as well as a substantial monetary investment. I do not wish to dissuade by expressing these facts, success is obtainable, but I do want to clear the air in terms of any delusions of grandeur that you may have acquired thus far in regard to retailing products on Amazon. Furthermore, I have not sold you this book in order to obtain your email address for the purposes of selling you other products or for signing you up for an expensive class. I would prefer my readers to be able to spend their money on setting up their business, creating a recognizable company, building an identifiable brand, sourcing their merchandise, effectively launching their products on Amazon, marketing their brands, and receiving a positive return on their investment. Therefore, I have written a one-stop shop straightforward systematic guide on how to properly conduct product discovery. It includes an in-depth, extensively researched, theory proven detailed research method written for you in the form of a step-by-step comprehensive walkthrough format that encompasses beginner, intermediate, and advanced Amazon Seller techniques. At the completion of this book you will have an intellectually deep understanding of the process of product discovery. You will learn (17) mathematical methods you can utilize in accordance with Amazon Seller software to conduct statistical data analysis to assist you in determining the level of third-party seller competition, (BSR), popularity among customers, projected per unit sales, and profitability margins in reference to any given keyword phrase or subcategory you are researching on Amazon. You will then be able to utilize this knowledge to repeatedly locate viable lucrative merchandise to retail on the Amazon Marketplace.

Although, I am providing you with the necessary keys to unlock the door to Amazon based e-commerce success your potential as an Amazon Seller all depends on the time, dedication, and monetary investment you will be putting towards growing your business. Please be aware, that if you remain devoted to extensively researching products, locating reputable suppliers, sourcing merchandise, building your brands, optimizing your Amazon product listings, properly marketing your goods, and to your customer base, the sky is the limit in terms of the extent you can grow as an Amazon Seller. Ultimately, the potential in which your business can flourish is going to depend on your willingness to put forth the necessary effort it takes to succeed. I hope for the very best results for each and every one of my readers. Without further ado lets teach you how to properly conduct product discovery.

Chapter 1:

Common Vocabulary, Acronyms, & Truncations Associated With Product Discovery As An Amazon Seller:

A crucial aspect to effectively learning how to properly conduct product discovery is to first become familiar with the dialect utilized by Amazon Sellers therefore I have provided a list of all applicable vocabulary, acronyms, and truncations associated with the language along with their respective definitions. Although, some of this vocabulary may be foreign to you, do not let that confuse or overwhelm you. The best way to view each one of these terms are as smaller puzzle pieces that form one large picture. As you progress through this book and the tutorials it contains they will all correctly snap into place. Upon the completion of this book you will be linguistically fluent and accustomed on how, when, and why to utilize the terminology.

❖ General Amazon Seller Terminology:

Amazon.com: An e-commerce retail marketplace platform that customers utilize to research, choose, and purchase numerous types of merchandise either directly from Amazon or from third-party Amazon Sellers. Commonly referred to as Amazon by retail consumers or as the Amazon Marketplace by third-party Amazon Sellers.

Third-Party Amazon Seller: Any individual or company independent of Amazon selling products on the Amazon Marketplace. Commonly referred to simply as an Amazon Seller.

(ASIN): Is an acronym for Amazon Standard Identification Number: A ten digit alphanumeric set of characters issued by Amazon and used to individually identify each product sold on the Amazon Marketplace.

(UPC/EAN): Is an acronym for Universal Product Code or European Article Number: A barcode utilized to identify and track each unit of merchandise. Whether an Amazon Seller is opting for (FBM) or (FBA) product fulfillment method a (UPC) is required to create their Amazon listing. UPCs can be acquired from a third-party company known as GS1.

(SKU): Is an acronym for Stock Keeping Unit: A unique numbered barcode issued by Amazon or the Seller themselves to individually identify their products & keep their merchandise organized in accordance with their Amazon Seller Central account.

(FNSKU): Is an acronym for Fulfillment Network Stock Keeping Unit: A unique numbered barcode issued by Amazon for Amazon Sellers to individually identify their products in accordance with their Amazon Seller Central account when utilizing the (FBA) product fulfillment method.

Stock-Out: Being entirely out of stock to sell.

Seasonality & Seasonal: When a particular product primarily sells during one of the four seasons. Winter, Spring, Summer, or Fall. For example, Christmas holiday decorations experience seasonality in regard to the fact that they typically only sell during the fall season.

Buy Box: The Amazon Buy Box aka "Add to Cart" button is a virtual shopping cart which is located on the right-hand side of all Amazon product listings. As you can observe in the following screenshot, within the buy box a customer shopping on Amazon can choose the unit quantity they wish to purchase. They can then either opt to add the product to their virtual shopping cart and continue shopping on Amazon or they can opt to "Buy Now." Amazon only chooses one seller to be featured in the Buy Box per sale. Since many sellers can retail the same merchandise on one product listing on Amazon, they often have to compete to be the featured Buy Box winner. Ultimately, winning the Buy Box simply means Amazon has chosen to feature your product. The other sellers of a particular product can be located in other areas within the product listing or directly below the Buy Box. Competing for the Buy Box happens more often with Retail Arbitragers & Wholesalers in contrast to Private Labelers who have a unique product and a well-built brand.

Image: Buy Box

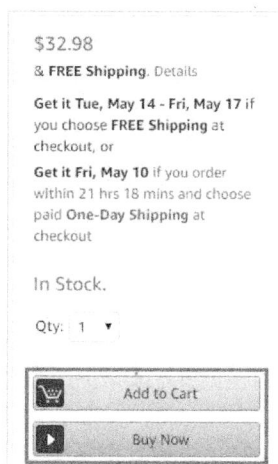

$32.98
& **FREE Shipping**. Details

Get it Tue, May 14 - Fri, May 17 if you choose **FREE Shipping** at checkout, or

Get it Fri, May 10 if you order within 21 hrs 18 mins and choose paid **One-Day Shipping** at checkout

In Stock.

Qty: 1 ▾

Add to Cart

Buy Now

Product Commingling: The act of selling (2) or more products together under one listing as a kit or whole package.

Amazon Product Categories: For the convenience of Amazon Customers and for Amazon database organizational purposes Amazon's webpage is broken up into categories titled by the types of products they contain.

Amazon Product Subcategories: For the convenience of Amazon Customers and for Amazon database organizational purposes Amazon's product categories are broken down into subcategories titled by the specific types of products they contain. For example, if a customer was searching for yoga related products they would first search the categories section on Amazon and locate the "Sports & Outdoors" category. They would then locate the subcategory titled "Exercise & Fitness." Within this subcategory they would find all yoga related products for sale.

(BSR): Is an acronym for Best Seller Rank: The rank an Amazon Seller's product listing is within the particular category they retail. A BSR of (1) means that an Amazon Seller's product listing is ranked #1 within the particular category or subcategory that it resides. This means that when an Amazon customer searches within that specific product category or subcategory the very first product listing on the very first page of listings will be the #1 (BSR) ranked Amazon Sellers. A BSR of (10) means that an Amazon Sellers product is ranked #10 within the product category that it resides. This means that when an Amazon customer searches within that specific product category the tenth product listing down on the very first page of listings will be the #10th (BSR) ranked Amazon Sellers, so on and so forth.

❖ <u>Amazon Product Listing Terminology:</u>

Amazon Search Engine & A9: Amazon has one computerized database containing all the merchandise they carry on their retail platform. The products are catalogued within their database by categories, subcategories, keywords, and keyword phrases so that they can easily be located by Amazon customers when they are searched for. When a consumer uses the search bar aka Amazon Search Engine within Amazon to locate a product to purchase they do so by entering specific keywords or keyword phrases that are relevant to the merchandise they are searching for. Amazon's A9 algorithm then mechanically scans, reads, and analyzes the customer's search terms to generate a list of applicable product listings in relation to the keywords the consumer utilized to perform their search.

Keywords & Keyword Phrases: These are the specific words or phrases that an Amazon Seller utilizes within the title, bullet points, description, and backend of their product listing to assist them in generating Amazon Search Engine visibility. Ultimately, Amazon Seller's utilize keywords and keyword phrases that directly correlate with the type of merchandise they retail so that their product listing is correctly catalogued within the Amazon database and recognized by Amazon's A9 algorithm.

Indexing Keywords: The act of an Amazon Seller's product listing keywords and keyword phrases being correctly recognized by Amazon's A9 algorithm when consumers utilize the Amazon Search Engine.

Title: The keywords and keyword phrases located at the top of an Amazon Seller's product listing that briefly describes the type of merchandise for sale.

Bullet Points: Each Amazon Seller can add up to (5) bullet points to their product listing. In contrast to the title of an Amazon listing the bullet points will typically include informative highlights that outline the products special features, its intended use, and the benefits of owning the merchandise. The bullet points are located underneath the price, size, and color option sections on an Amazon product listing.

Image: As you can observe in the screenshot below, the title is located at the top of the Amazon Seller's product listing followed by (5) descriptive bullet points located below the price, size, and color variations sections:

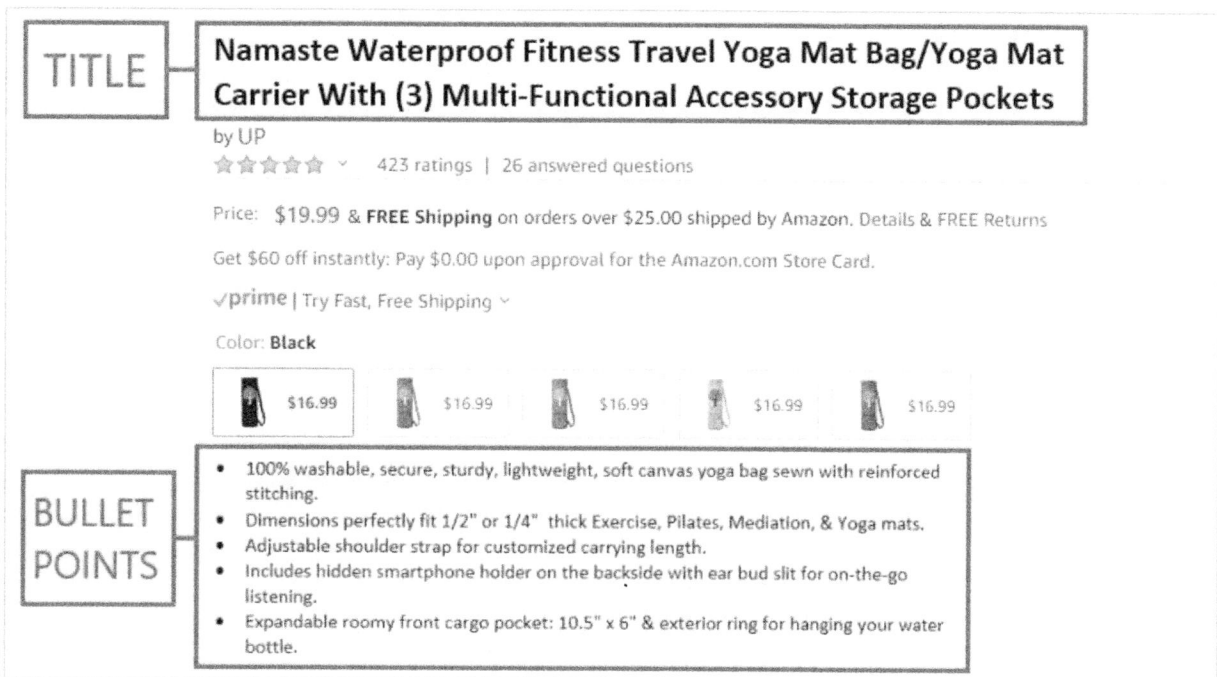

Description: This is the section of an Amazon Seller's product listing that is utilized to showcase their products purpose and functionality in extensive detail to the customer. Furthermore, the description can be used to communicate the Amazon Seller's brand history and company values.

Backend: This is the section of an Amazon Seller's product listing that is utilized specifically for (SEO), keyword indexing, and phrase matching purposes. The keywords added to this section are not visible to the customer shopping on Amazon.

Product Listing Optimization: The act of making necessary alterations to a product listing so that it is functioning to the best of its ability and properly indexing on Amazon.

Amazon (SERP): Is an acronym for Search Engine Rank Position: When a consumer uses the search bar aka Amazon Search Engine within Amazon to locate a product to purchase they do so by entering specific keywords or keyword phrases that are relevant to the merchandise they are searching for. Amazon's A9 algorithm then mechanically scans, reads, and analyzes the customer's search terms to generate a list of applicable product listings in relation to the keywords the consumer utilized to perform their search. If an Amazon Seller is indexed for the particular keyword or keyword phrase that the customer searched for then the seller's product listing will appear in the generated list, but there may be several pages of product listings. What page an Amazon Seller's product listing appears on is known as the Search Engine Rank Position. For example, if an Amazon Seller is ranking on page #1 for a specific indexed keyword that means that when a customer performs a search for a product on Amazon utilizing that particular keyword the seller's product listing will be located somewhere on the first page of generated results seen by the consumer. If per say an Amazon Seller's (SERP) is (4) then they will appear all the way on the 4th page of generated product listing results thus being much less visible and more difficult to locate by the Amazon customer.

❖ Amazon Advertising & Sales Terminology:

(AD): Is acronym for Advertising: Any act of promoting and marketing a product or service through a print advertisement or commercial advertisement.

Amazon (PPC): Is acronym for Pay Per Click: (PPC) operates in direct correlation with Sponsored Ads. When an Amazon Seller creates a Sponsored Ad campaign they are charged a designated amount each time an Amazon customer clicks on the Sponsored Ad and is directed to the seller's particular product listing. Ultimately, the Amazon Seller is paying to appear on page #1 within their specific product category instead of attempting to solely rank organically thus inorganically driving traffic to their product listing.

Amazon Sponsored Ad: The act of an Amazon Seller paying for their merchandise to be advertised on Amazon in direct correlation to the relevant indexed keywords or keyword phrases they utilize in the copy of their product listing or manually select to bid on. The Amazon Seller then pays a designated amount anytime a customer clicks on the Sponsored Ad and is directed to the seller's particular product listing. Ultimately, the Amazon Seller is paying to have their product listing appear on page #1 within their specific product category instead of attempting to solely rank organically thus inorganically driving traffic to their listing.

Image: As you can observe in the screenshot below, when a (PPC) Sponsored Ad appears in the customer's generated search results it clearly states directly on the listing that it is a "Sponsored" product:

Sponsored ⓘ
Polarized Classic Aviator Sunglasses for Men and Women 100% UV...
★★★★☆ ⌄ 53
$19⁹⁹
FREE Shipping on orders over $25 shipped by Amazon

❖ Product Fulfillment Terminology:

(Amazon Product Fulfillment Center): This is the warehouse that Amazon Seller's send their goods when utilizing Amazon's (FBA) program. This storage, preparation, and shipping facility is commonly referred to as the (FBA) warehouse.

(FBA): Is an acronym for Fulfilled By Amazon: An Amazon Seller will send their merchandise for their listing to an Amazon Fulfillment Center where it will be stored until sold. When a sale is made from the Amazon Seller's product listing Amazon picks, packs, and ships the product to the customer. There are various fees associated with this procedure commonly known as (FBA) fees.

Amazon (FBA) Fees: When utilizing the (FBA) product fulfillment method these are the fees that Amazon charges to pick, pack, and ship an Amazon Seller's merchandise to their customers. These fees substantially vary depending on the dimensions and weight of the product in question.

Amazon Referral Fees: Per sale fee charged to Amazon Sellers. Amazon will typically retains approximately (15%) of an Amazon Seller's retail price per unit sold.

(FBM) aka (MFN): Is an acronym for Fulfilled By Merchant aka Merchant Fulfilled Network: An Amazon Seller will store their own merchandise until sold. When a sale is made from the Amazon Seller's product listing the seller is in charge of picking, packing, and shipping their merchandise to the consumer.

❖ Internet, Computer, & Software Terminology:

App: This is a truncated form of saying software application. It is typically utilized by smartphone users to refer to software applications they download to their device.

(MAC): This is a truncated form of referring to either an Apple branded Macintosh laptop or Macintosh home/desktop computer.

(PC): This is a truncated from of referring to a personal computer. It can refer to a laptop or home/desktop computer. It is typically used in reference to any computer other than an Apple branded Macintosh.

(AI): Is an acronym for Adobe Illustrator which is a purchasable Adobe program. (AI) is a vector based computer software program that comes preloaded with hundreds of font choices, colors, shapes, and drawing tools for designing logos, brand names, and graphics. It allows an individual to design their own illustrations from scratch for their company and products.

(AF): Is an acronym for Art File: To effectively brand/private label products manufacturers will require an Art File containing the specific font/color of a primary company name, brand name, and brand logo, such as one would create in Adobe Illustrator. Manufacturers will commonly refer to an (AI) Adobe Illustrator as an (AF) Art File.

(PDF): Is an acronym for Portable Document Format: A pdf is a universally readable file format that can be electronically sent. The pdf can contain text, images, and graphics. When sourcing products from manufacturers some suppliers may not have the capabilities required to view a particular image or document that is sent due to the fact that they do not have the same software available to them as an Amazon Seller therefore they will require the file to be formatted and alternatively sent as a pdf. For example, some manufacturers will not be able to properly view an (AI) File. They will then request a pdf version of the document. Most computer files, images, and graphics can typically be saved as a pdf copy of the original.

❖ Financial Terminology:

E-commerce: Is an acronym for electronic commerce: The act of conducting transactions digitally via the Internet for goods or services.

Product Price Point: The amount an Amazon Seller retails their product for.

Landing Costs: This is the total sum of all costs associated with manufacturing, branding, packaging, labeling, & shipping a product until it arrives to the Amazon Fulfillment Center hence the landing aspect of the term.

Gross Profit aka Profit Margin: This is the total amount of income a company or individual generates from retailing their merchandise after deducting all expenses associated with production, such as manufacturing, branding, packaging, shipping, storage, and marketing. Furthermore, an Amazon Seller would also factor in such expenses as Amazon (FBA) fees. To receive a gross profit total, an Amazon Seller would deduct all production, FBA fees, and marketing costs from their overall sales revenue.

Quarterly: A period of time based on three calendar months. Amazon Sellers typically order their merchandise and review their financials on a (3) month quarterly period time scale.

Standard Quarterly Period Months:

- Quarter 1: January, February, March
- Quarter 2: April, May, June
- Quarter 3: July, August, September
- Quarter 4: October, November, December

Annually: A period of time that refers to once a year. Annually=Yearly

❖ <u>Product Inspection Terminology:</u>

Third-Party Inspection: This is a hirable service offered by various companies that send a product inspector to a supplier's location to evaluate the quality of a buyer's products either during production and after or solely post manufacturing of their mass order. The inspector will be provided with a (QC) checklist from the buyer which they will utilize to evaluate the product for items, such as:

- Unit quantity.
- To confirm that the supplier did not deviate from the buyer provided (QC) checklist.
- To confirm that the product is not defective, damaged, or scratched.
- To confirm that the correct (HS) codes are on the shipping labels and documents.
- To confirm that the correct customs safety and regulatory certification codes are on the shipping labels and documents.
- To confirm that the product is properly and securely packaged for shipping.

❖ Product Discovery Terminology:

Target Market: Some Amazon Sellers prefer to begin or center their product research utilizing a method known as identifying a target market wherein they aim at selling products that fulfill a specific group of customer's individual focused needs.

Niche Product Category: Relating to a specific product subset of a larger general product category.

Niche Product Example:

Product Category: Fishing
Niche Market: Ice Fishing Products
Niche Product: Neoprene Ice Fishing Gloves With Battery Powered Hand Warmers

❖ Product Research & Manufacturer Terminology:

(B2B): Is an acronym for Business To Business: For example, when an Amazon Seller sources products from a manufacturer that would be known as a business to business transaction.

Product Sourcing: The act an Amazon Seller performs to locate a supplier to sell already produced products or to have the supplier manufacture products.

Product Specifications: Any specifications an Amazon Seller requests to a supplier in regard to a product, including but not limited to dimensions, color, materials used in manufacture, specific branding, and product packaging.

Product Variations: Any variations, such as a difference in dimensions or color of the same product an Amazon Seller retails on their product listing. For example, if an Amazon Seller retails a specific yoga mat but offers it in (4) different colors that would mean that they carry (4) variations of the product.

Added Feature: This is the process of adding a new attribute to an already existing product, such as an exterior smartphone charging port to a messenger bag.

Mass Order: When an Amazon Seller has decided that their sample order from a supplier meets the quality standards that they require they will then move forward with the production of a large order of units known as a Mass Order.

Product Discovery: The act of a retailer aggressively searching for viable profitable products to sell on the Amazon Marketplace.

(PL): Is an acronym for Private Label: The act of a retailer printing their primary company name, brand name, and brand logo on a pre-invented already existing product. Ultimately, the products are sold with the retailer's primary company name, brand name, and brand logo printed on them instead of the inventors/manufacturers.

❖ <u>Product Branding & Legal Intellectual Property Protection Terminology:</u>

Branding: The act of a company adding their primary company name, brand name, and brand logo to a product and its packaging.

TM: Is an acronym for Trademark: The act of a company legally registering any words, marks, and color combinations associated with their primary company name, brand name, brand symbols, or brand logo to protect the integrity of their brand from being reproduced by another company.

Patent: The act of a company legally registering their invention with the proper government authority to protect their product idea from being reproduced and sold by another company.

❖ <u>Amazon Product Listing Customer Feedback Terminology:</u>

Product Listing Review: Amazon customers can choose to write a product evaluation directly on an Amazon Seller's product listing in regard to the specific merchandise they purchased.

Product Listing Star Rating System: Amazon customers can choose to evaluate a product utilizing a star rating system directly on an Amazon Seller's product listing for the specific merchandise they purchased.

- **(1)** Star Rating=The lowest negative product feedback rating an Amazon Seller's product listing can receive.
- **(5)** Star Rating=The highest positive product feedback rating an Amazon Seller's product listing can receive.

(ERP): Is an acronym for Amazon Early Reviewer Program: For a fee of ($60) per, Amazon Sellers can opt to enroll their (SKUs) into the Early Reviewer Program which is an incentivized review service designed and offered by Amazon that will assist them in acquiring up to (5) authentic customer reviews/star ratings for their product listings. Once the seller has enrolled a (SKU) in the program Amazon will choose, at random, up to (5) customers who have purchased their merchandise to write an honest authentic review and leave a star rating directly on their product listing in exchange for a ($3) Amazon gift card.

*Understanding the dialect associated with product discovery is a significant essential milestone in successfully researching and locating viable profitable merchandise to retail on the Amazon Marketplace.

To-Do List Chapter 1:

- o Familiarize Yourself With Amazon Seller Dialect & Terminology.

Chapter 2:

Helium 10: A Suite Of Software Tools Specifically Designed For Use By Amazon Sellers:

Helium 10: www.helium10.com

Choosing, understanding, and operating the best Amazon Seller software is a key component to success. There are numerous types of software companies that offer various tools for Amazon Sellers, but after much research into each type, individual trial and error with them, I ultimately chose to utilize Helium 10 for my business necessities. Helium 10 offers a complete set of software tools with unique features all found in one location for an affordable monthly membership fee and they prove to be the most accurate with the Amazon analytics they provide. The software suite is solely based on routinely updated data from current Amazon product listings which can be used for product discovery, determining product profitability, tracking competition, launching products, and calculating (FBA) fees. The software also offers their users the ability to research their competitor's product listings for valuable keywords so that they can effectively build, maintain, and advertise their own product listings. Furthermore, Helium 10 operates in accordance with the user's Amazon Seller Central Account by allowing them to track, record, and organize their keywords so that they can easily evaluate their keyword search volume and optimize their product listings accordingly. The software suite also offers protection features as well, such as the ability to assist Amazon Sellers in tracking and receiving reimbursements for money Amazon may owe them for any errors Amazon has made, alerts the user to hijackers on their product listings, and protects the user's inventory by allowing them to set limits on promotional coupons. The software also contains an automated email tool that connects directly with the user's Amazon Seller Central account that allows them to easily conduct post purchase customer follow-up. Essentially, Helium 10 is an online software platform that provides an extensive suite of tools for Amazon Sellers that are simple to learn, use, and implement into building and maintaining their Amazon business.

Downloading/Installing/Signing Into The Google Chrome Web Browser:

If you do not currently have it on your (PC) or (Mac) computer you will need to download the Google Chrome Web Browser via the provided address, create a Google account, and sign into it. Google Chrome is essential for operating the Amazon Seller product research tool Xray provided by Helium 10, which is a Google Chrome Extension, and will be utilized throughout the remainder of this book for conducting product discovery.

*Note: Xray only functions within a Google Chrome Web Browser via computer.

The List Below Contains The Logo, Title, Type, Description, & Explanation On The Utilization Of Each Of The (16) Tools Offered By Helium 10:

Black Box
Amazon Product Research

1. Black Box: This software tool operates as an Amazon research tool utilized to assist you in conducting product discovery by allowing you to enter specific criteria within the provided filter's section. After selecting detailed filters, the software searches the Amazon database and generates a list of merchandise that is currently retailing on Amazon in relation to the specific criteria you entered. The generated list contains an image of the product, the specific (ASIN) associated with the merchandise, product listing information, number of sellers, product price point, monthly sales, monthly revenue, (BSR), and review volume.

Trendster
Amazon Trends Finder

2. Trendster: This software operates as a product seasonality reference tool wherein you can determine if the merchandise you are investigating primarily retails in particular times of the year in contrast to year round.

Magnet^2
Keyword Research

3. Magnet: This software tool operates as an Amazon keyword locater by allowing you to search a particular keyword or keyword phrase. Magnet then generates a list containing all relevant keywords associated with your particular search which you can then use to comprise your own list of valuable traffic driving keywords to utilize when building your product listing.

Cerebro
Reverse ASIN Lookup

4. Cerebro: This software tool operates in a similar manner as Magnet, but with Cerebro you are searching and evaluating the keyword analytics of one or more specific (ASINs) at a time. This tool assists you in understanding your top competitor's keyword tactics and indexing approach. From your investigation you can comprise your own list of valuable traffic driving keywords to utilize when building your product listing.

Frankenstein
Keyword Processor

5. Frankenstein: This software operates as a tool for efficiently building a highly optimized product listing by working as a keyword processor that creates a structured document for the Amazon keywords you discover in your research. Essentially, it exports your top competitor's keywords into an easy to read format which you can organize accordingly and prepare for import into your product listing.

Scribbles
Listing Optimizer

6. Scribbles: This software operates as a tool for efficiently building a highly optimized product listing by allowing you to import your keywords and keyword phrases directly from Frankenstein. You can utilize Scribbles to write each aspect of your product listing including the title, bullet points, description, and backend.

Index Checker
Keyword Index Checker

7. Index Checker: This software operates as a product listing optimization tool that makes sure the keywords and keyword phrases located in your product listing are properly indexing. If you find that your keywords are not indexing you can optimize your product listing by rearranging the location of the keywords or interchanging the unindexed keywords with keywords that you believe will index which will fundamentally help you rank to the top of page one of customer generated search results within the category you are retailing.

Keyword Tracker
Product Rank Tracking

8. Keyword Tracker: This software operates as a tool utilized to track your product listing keyword page rankings on Amazon. Ultimately, this software application allows you to track the page you are ranking on in direct relation to the keywords utilized in your product listing. If you find that the keywords you are tracking are ranking beyond page one of customer generated search results you can make the necessary changes to optimize your product listing by replacing the non-traffic driving keywords with higher ranking keywords.

Alerts
Listing Monitoring

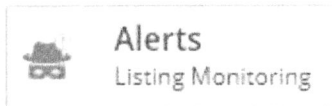

9. Alerts: This software tool operates as an alarm system that alerts you to anyone who may be attempting to utilize your product listing and is winning your buy box by retailing either your merchandise, or counterfeit versions of such, without your knowledge and prior consent to do so.

Inventory Protector
Coupon Abuse Prevention

10. Inventory Protector: This software operates as a tool that protects your inventory by allowing you to easily and quickly set limits on the number of units an Amazon customer can purchase from your product listing. This tool is specifically useful when you are retailing your merchandise at a promotional discounted rate for a limited time. When you do not set limits on the amount of purchases each customer can obtain when you are running a promotion on your product listing you run the risk of selling all of your products at a discounted rate to one individual who may only be purchasing the merchandise to resell the goods at a higher rate. Ultimately, setting unit purchase limits through utilization of Inventory Protector allows you to prevent retail arbitragers from purchasing your entire allotted discounted stock solely in order to retail it for a higher price directly on your product listing, Amazon, or alternative marketplaces.

Refund Genie
Reimbursement Assistance

11. Refund Genie: This software tool operates as a tracking reimbursement service that protects your Amazon Seller Account balance by compiling a list of refunds that Amazon owes you for errors in regard to damaged or lost products.

Misspellinator
Misspellings Checker

12. Misspellinator: This software operates as a tool that finds the most commonly misspelled keywords that Amazon customers will occasionally type into the Amazon Search Engine when attempting to locate the type of merchandise you retail. You can then add these unique misspellings to the backend of your product listings in an attempt to generate higher customer traffic volume to your product listing.

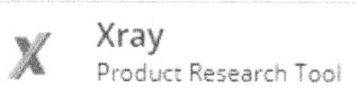
Xray
Product Research Tool

13. Xray: This Google Chrome Extension software tool operates in direct accordance with Amazon by functioning as an analytical statistical product research tool that allows you to view and evaluate data on each product listing you locate when you are conducting product discovery. Furthermore, Xray can be utilized to pin the products you are interested in retailing which are then saved into an organized list within your Helium 10 account for later review. Ultimately, Xray is an extremely valuable product research tool that should be heavily utilized when you are conducting product discovery.

Xray Provides The Following List Of Product Listing Data:

- (ASIN)
- Brand Name
- Product Listing Title
- Product Category
- Buy Box Ownership
- # of Sellers
- Fulfillment Type
- (FBA) Fee
- Daily/Monthly/Tri-Yearly, & Yearly Sales
- Monthly Revenue
- (BSR)
- Product Listing Star Rating
- Product Listing Review Count
- Product Listing Review Velocity
- Product Dimensions
- Product Weight
- Product Size Tier
- # Of Images The Product Listing Has
-

The Helium 10 Google Chrome Extension Also Provides (5) Additional Research Tools:

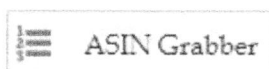
ASIN Grabber

1) (ASIN) Grabber: This keyword research tool organizes all the Amazon product listings from a particular page within a specific category into an easily readable list in order from highest ranked to least ranked.

(ASIN) Grabber Provides Valuable Information For Each Product Listing:

- Page Rank Position
- (ASIN)
- Brand Name
- Product Listing Title
- Product Price Point
- (BSR)
- Product Listing Star Rating
- Product Listing Review Volume

Ultimately, (ASIN) Grabber can be used to investigate your competitor's listings when conducting keyword research. You can then utilize the information the tool provides to determine the highest ranked product listings. You can then easily grab the top (5) competitor's (ASINs) and enter them into Cerebro to run a reverse (ASIN) search which will assist you in locating valuable, relevant, and explanatory keywords to utilize when building your product listing.

Image: (ASIN) Grabber being utilized in the Men's Sunglasses category on Amazon:

# ▲ ASIN	Brand	Title	Price	BSR	Rating	Reviews
1 B00SMRN88Y	DUCO	SP DUCO Mens Sports Polarized Sunglasses UV Protection Sunglasses for Men 8177s	$22.00	486	4.5	4,273
2 B07D7VX8MT	SUNGAIT	SP SUNGAIT Ultra Lightweight Rectangular Polarized Sunglasses UV400 Protection	$14.99	125	4.5	896
3 B07LG6KTTS	OLIEYE	OLIEYE Rectangular Polarized Sunglasses for Men 100% UV protection	$22.99	28,512	4	35
4 B07LG65716	OLIEYE	OLIEYE Retro Unisex Polarized Sunglasses for Men/Women-100% UV protection	$28.99	43,643	4	29
5 B07LG6NF5W	OLIEYE	OLIEYE Men HD Polarized Driving Sunglasses for Men-Classic Square Sunglasses	$21.99	17,981	4	57
6 B07647Z4YQ	Obsidian-Sunglasses	Obsidian Sunglasses for Women or Men Polarized Square Frame 04	$23.40	69,161	4.5	32
7 B01M311ACN	MERRYS	MERRY'S Unisex Polarized Aluminum Sunglasses Vintage Sun Glasses For Men/Women S8286	$12.29	46	4.5	4,150
8 B01LYQK0YX	SUNGAIT	SUNGAIT Ultra Lightweight Rectangular Polarized Sunglasses UV400 Protection	$14.99	125	4.5	2,264
9 B07K7BVXZG	FEIDU	Polarized Sunglasses for Men Retro - FEIDU Polarized Retro Sunglasses for Men FD2149	$11.99	1,257	4.5	359
10 B019MM7XVK	RIVBOS	RIVBOS Polarized Sports Sunglasses Driving Glasses Shades for Men Women T690 Unbreakabl...	$19.98	185	4.5	2,142
11 B01C9ZOVX0	Joopin	Joopin Semi-Rimless Polarized Sunglasses Women Men Retro Brand Sun Glasses	$12.29	136	4.5	4,845
12 B01SRZNQ3M	Hulislem	Hulislem S1 Sport Polarized Sunglasses FDA Approved	$18.59	291	4.5	2,398
13 B07MW7BBX5	KALIYADI	Polarized Sunglasses for Men and Women	Semi-Rimless Frame	Driving Sun glasses	100% ...	$19.99	274	4.5	463

% Profitability Calculator

2) Profitability Calculator: This tool is utilized to investigate your competitor's individual product listings when conducting product discovery to assist you in determining if the item you are researching would be profitable for you to sell on the Amazon Marketplace. Ultimately, it calculates an approximated total to help you identify whether or not the specific merchandise you are evaluating is a viable lucrative product option for you to retail by providing a projected view of Net Profit, Profit Margin, and (ROI).

Profitability Calculator Provides Valuable Information:

- Exact Product Dimensions
- Exact Product Weight
- Outbound Shipping Weight
- (FBA) Tier Size
- Product Price Point
- Estimated (FBA) Storage Times
- Estimated Per Unit Manufacturing Cost
- Estimated Freight Cost
- Per Unit Freight Cost
- (FBA) Storage Fee
- Amazon Referral Fee

Image: Profitability Calculator being utilized in the Men's Sunglasses category on a product by a company named Iconic:

Inventory Levels

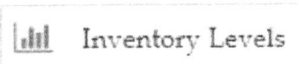

3) Inventory Levels: This tool allows you to research your competitor's individual product listing inventory levels. When your competitors are out of stock consumers can no longer order from them which may mean that you will experience an increase in sales volume if you own a similar product listing. By tracking your competitor's stock levels you can be sure to increase your stock if necessary when they are running low.

Image: Inventory Levels tool being utilized in the Men's Sunglasses category on a product by a company named Iconic. As you can observe in the screenshot below, this particular product has a current stock of (677) on Amazon:

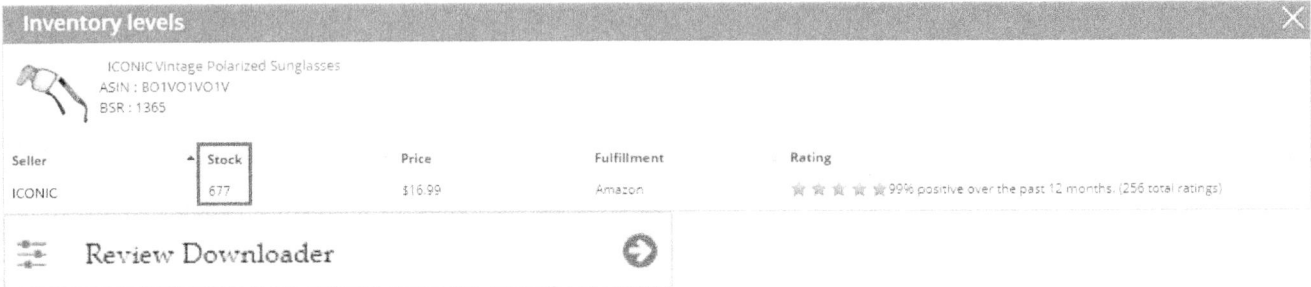

Inventory levels

ICONIC Vintage Polarized Sunglasses
ASIN : BO1VO1VO1V
BSR : 1365

Seller	Stock	Price	Fulfillment	Rating
ICONIC	677	$16.99	Amazon	⭐⭐⭐⭐⭐ 99% positive over the past 12 months. (256 total ratings)

Review Downloader →

4) Review Downloader: This tool allows you to easily and quickly download your competitor's individual product listing reviews. It is beneficial to investigate your competitor's reviews when you are conducting product discovery to assist you in gaining insight into what the consumers are saying about a particular product. If you can identify negative features about a competitor's product prior to you manufacturing something similar you can then opt to make the necessary alterations to satisfy consumers. By utilizing this technique and selling an enhanced better developed higher quality product than that of your competitors you could end up dominating the category you are retailing in.

Helium 10 Pro Training

5) Helium 10 Pro Training: This is a direct link to various Online tutorials that teach the how to effectively utilize Helium 10's suite of software tools.

To Download The Helium 10 Google Chrome Extension, follow the instructional steps included with the labeled images below:

Step #1: Launch the Google Chrome Web Browser.

Step #2: Using your mouse, left-click and release on the Google Apps icon located on the left-hand side of the screen:

New Tab ✕

G |

Apps | Amazon | Helium 10

Step #3: Using your mouse, left-click and release on the Google Chrome Web Store navigational task button:

Step #4: Type Helium 10 into the Chrome Web Store search bar and then press the Enter key (PC) or Return key (Mac):

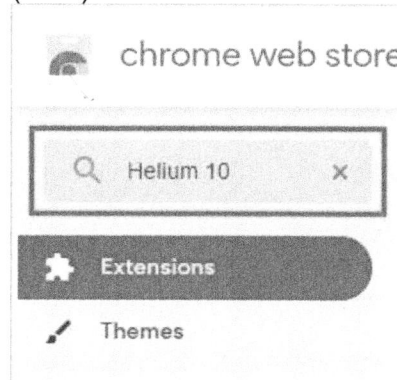

Step #5: Using your mouse, left-click and release on the "Add to Chrome" navigational task button:

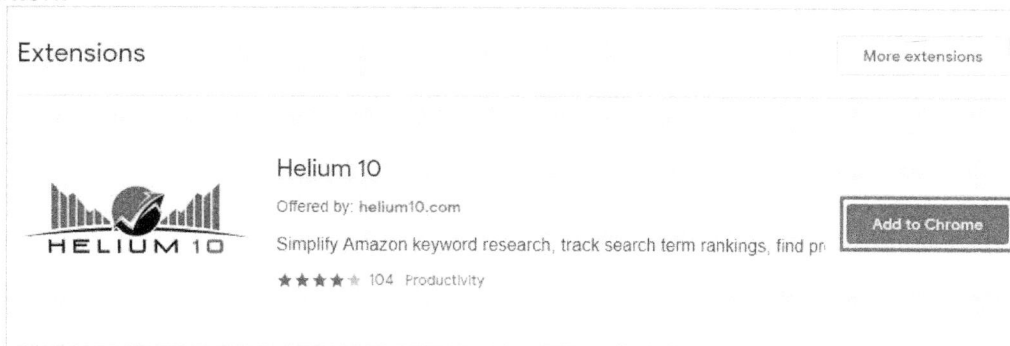

Step #6: Using your mouse, left-click and release on the "Add extension" task button:

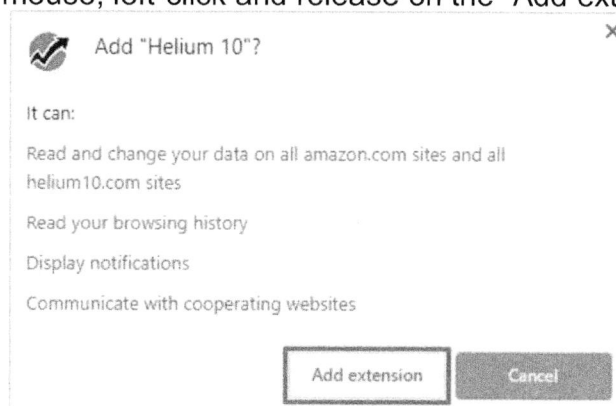

Step #7: You will now observe that the Helium 10 Google Chrome Extension icon has been added to the Google Chrome Web Browser toolbar:

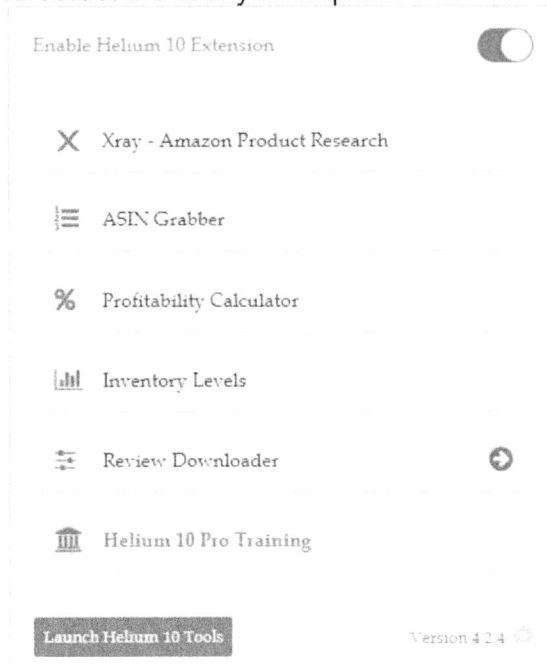

*To launch the Helium 10 Google Chrome Extension toolbar when conducting product discovery on Amazon and utilize the (6) tools that accompany the extension simply use your mouse, left-click on the Helium 10 icon located in the Google Chrome Web Browser toolbar and select the tool you require:

Profits
Financial Analytics Dashboard

14. Profits: This software tool operates in accordance with your Amazon product listings to track and record your profits, units sold, and inventory levels. It gives you the data of daily, weekly, monthly, and yearly gross/net profits. Ultimately, by tracking your daily sales trends, you can observe whether each product listing you own is increasing or declining in profit.

❖ As you can observe in the screenshot below, Profits can be located on the top of the Helium 10 dashboard:

PROFITS

Follow-Up
Email Automation Tool

15. Follow-Up: This software connects directly with your Amazon Seller Central account and operates as an automated follow-up email tool that that allows you to contact customers post purchase.

❖ As you can observe from the screenshot below, Follow-Up can be located on the top of the Helium 10 dashboard:

FOLLOW-UP

16. Evaluation Result: This software operates in direct correlation with Amazon and allows you easily examine your competitors to observe their overall product listing optimization level. You can utilize this information to build an equally optimized or a more enhanced product listing than that of your competitors.

Evaluation Result Provides Valuable Competitor Product Listing Information:

- Number Of Images
- Main Image Background
- Image Pixel Dimensions
- Title Character Count
- Number Of Bullet Points
- Description Character Count
- Star Rating
- Review Volume

To Locate Helium 10's Individual Product Evaluation Tool, follow the instructional steps included with the labeled images below:

Step #1: Make sure that you are subscribed to Helium 10's Free, Platinum, Diamond, or Elite Plan and that you are signed into your Helium 10 account via your (PC) or (Mac). Please note, that membership types and pricing plans can be observed in the following section.

Step #2: Navigate to www.amazon.com from within the Google Chrome Web Browser:

Step #3: Search for a product of your choice on Amazon.

Step #4: Locate one product listing.

❖ As you can observe in the screenshot below, for this software tool example, I chose to utilize Men's Vintage Polarized Sunglasses by the company Iconic:

ICONIC Vintage Polarized Sunglasses
☆ ☆ ☆ ☆ ☆ ⌄ 446
$16⁹⁹ $29.99
FREE Shipping on orders over $25 shipped by Amazon

Step #5: Using your mouse, left-click and release anywhere on the product listing to navigate to the product details page.

Step #6: As you can observe in the screenshot below, you will see a blue Helium 10 "Evaluation Result" icon in the top left-hand corner of the product details page. The numbers located below the words "Evaluation result" represent the overall optimization level score of the product listing:

Evaluation result
9.41 of 10

- An evaluation of (10/10) is the highest score a product listing can receive. A high score indicates that the product listing is well-optimized, successfully built, and does not require improvements.
- An evaluation of (0/10) is the lowest score a product listing can receive. A low score indicates that the product listing is poorly optimized, unsuccessfully built, and requires improvements.

Step #7: Using your mouse, scroll, without clicking, over the top of the blue "Evaluation result" to generate the product listings statistical data information sheet. As you can observe from the screenshot below, Iconic has a product listing an excellent evaluation result of (9.41/10). The only issue with this product listing is the number of characters they utilized to write their title which is clearly highlighted in red. Ultimately, they could optimize their product listing by adding additional valuable keywords into their product listing title to enhance their indexing potential and search visibility on Amazon:

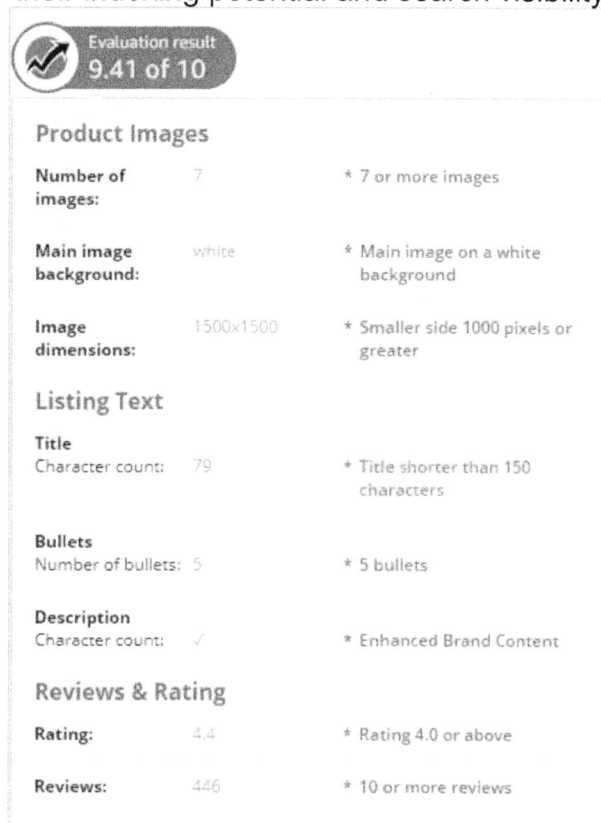

Evaluation result
9.41 of 10

Product Images

Number of images:	7	* 7 or more images
Main image background:	white	* Main image on a white background
Image dimensions:	1500x1500	* Smaller side 1000 pixels or greater

Listing Text

Title
| Character count: | 79 | * Title shorter than 150 characters |

Bullets
| Number of bullets: | 5 | * 5 bullets |

Description
| Character count: | ✓ | * Enhanced Brand Content |

Reviews & Rating

| Rating: | 4.4 | * Rating 4.0 or above |
| Reviews: | 446 | * 10 or more reviews |

An Explanation Of The Different Types Of Helium 10 Memberships & The Tools Each Provide Can Observed In The (2) Charts Below:

Helium 10 offers you a free trial period of the software suite so that you can determine if the tools will benefit you as an Amazon Seller. Once you complete this trial period, you can choose to subscribe to the services they offer by paying for tools Al La Carte or you can purchase a membership that allows access to the entire suite of tools.

Chart #1: Membership Options & Pricing:

Plans And Pricing

Free Plan	Platinum Plan	Diamond Plan	Elite Plan
$0	$97/month	$197/month	$397/month
The perfect way to get a taste of what Helium 10 has to offer.	The perfect entry-level solutions package for the everyday seller.	The best investment for advanced sellers with expanded limits and capabilities.	The highest-tier plan comes with cutting-edge training, in-person workshops, high-level networking, and full access to our tools.
Sign Up	Learn More	Learn More	Learn More

Chart #2: Tools & Number Of Uses Provided With Each Type Of Membership Plan:

Plan Comparison

	FREE PLAN $0 /month	A LA CARTE PLAN -/- /month	PLATINUM PLAN $97 /month	DIAMOND PLAN $197 /month	ELITE PLAN $397 /month
Black Box Amazon Product Research	20 uses	$37/month	⊘	⊘	⊘
Trendster Amazon Trends Finder	30 days	⊖	⊘	⊘	⊘
Magnet² Keyword Research	2 uses per day	$37/month	⊘	⊘	⊘
Cerebro Reverse ASIN Lookup	2 uses per day	$37/month	⊘	⊘	⊘
Frankenstein Keyword Processor	30 days	⊖	⊘	⊘	⊘
Scribbles Listing Optimizer	30 days	⊖	⊘	⊘	⊘
Index Checker Keyword Index Checker	6 uses	$17/month	150 uses/month	300 uses/month	500 uses/month
Keyword Tracker Product Rank Tracking	Up to 20 Keywords	$57/month	Up to 2,500 Keywords	Up to 5,000 Keywords	Up to 5,000 Keywords
Alerts Listing Monitoring	Up to 2 ASINs	$37/month	Up to 300 ASINs	Up to 600 ASINs	Up to 1,000 ASINs
Inventory Protector Coupon Abuse Prevention	⊘	⊘	⊘	⊘	⊘
Refund Genie Reimbursement Assistance	Limited	$97/month	⊘	⊘	⊘
Xray Product Research Tool	50 uses	$17/month	⊘	⊘	⊘
Profits Financial Analytics Dashboard	30 days	$37/month	⊘	⊘	⊘
Follow-Up Email Automation Tool	⊖	⊖	5,000 emails/month	15,000 emails/month	50,000 emails/month
Multi-User Login Create Limited Access Users	⊖	⊖	⊖	⊘	⊘

By viewing the chart on pricing and types of memberships, you can observe that there are only (4) key differences in the functionality of the Helium 10 software within the Platinum, Diamond, & Elite Plan memberships.

These Differences Include:

- The Quantity Of Uses Per Month For Index Checker
- Number Of Keywords That Can Be Tracked
- Number Of (ASIN) Alerts
- Number Of Users That Can Login Into Your Account
- Number Of Follow-Up Emails You Can Send On A Monthly Basis

The type of subscription you choose should reflect on two primary factors; personal preference in terms of what you believe you will need to function, grow, and effectively maintain your presence as an Amazon Seller as well as your monthly budget for Amazon Seller tools. From my experience as an Amazon Seller I have found the Platinum Plan to be the most sufficient and affordable type of membership for my e-commerce Amazon ventures. It includes all of the tools that Helium 10 offers with an adequate amount of uses and as I am the sole operator of the software I do not have a need for multiple users to login. If you are initially building your company on a larger scale with an exceptional number of (ASINs) and several employees requiring multiple-user logins to one shared Helium 10 account then I recommend the Diamond or Elite Plan membership option. If you decide after your free trial period that you will only utilize a few tools then opting for the Al La Carte method of membership may better suite your business needs. Please note that you can always upgrade your plan from Al La Carte to Platinum to Diamond to Elite as your business grows.

Helium 10 is an integral piece of solving the Amazon puzzle and excelling as an Amazon Seller. After learning and implementing these tools into your business you will be able to utilize the Amazon statistical data they provide to locate viable profitable merchandise to retail, perform valuable keyword research, build well-optimized product listings, efficiently advertise your product listings, and properly maintain healthy product listings. Effectively utilizing Helium 10's suite of tools can lead to an increase in customer traffic to your product listings ultimately resulting in substantial sales volume. Essentially, if it is economically feasible for you to become a member and subscribe I would highly recommend Helium 10 due to its dynamic functionality for Amazon Sellers. So that you attain a better understanding of how to utilize Helium 10 I will be referring to the use of the software throughout Chapter 3.

To create your Helium 10 account and begin your free trial launch the Google Chrome Web Browser and navigate to www.helium10.com. Click on the free trial icon and they will guide you through the sign up process.

*Note: If any issues arise regarding the use of your Helium 10 account their support team can be reached via telephone at **1 (949) 943-3142** or via email at support@helium10.com.

Although, I opt to utilize Helium 10 due to the accuracy of data it provides and the functionality of the numerous tools it offers, there are other options from several companies that retail similar Amazon Seller software. For your convenience I have provided a list below containing the most popular software alternatives for you to research so that you can compare and contrast their differences. Upon evaluation of the alternative options in the provided list below you can acquire a better understanding of why I choose to utilize Helium 10 in comparison to other software available to Amazon Sellers. Furthermore, by examining the list below you will understand the alternative software on the market so that if you consult with other Amazon Sellers and they reference one of the companies listed when they explain the techniques they utilize you will comprehend what they are referring to.

1) Jungle Scout: www.junglescout.com

2) Sellics: www.sellics.com

3) amazeowl: www.amazeowl.com

4) AMZScout: www.amzscout.com

5) Viral Launch: www.virallaunch.com

　　*Understanding how to utilize Helium 10 is another significant essential milestone in successfully researching and locating viable profitable merchandise to retail on the Amazon Marketplace.

To-Do List Chapter 2:

- ○ Create A Free Account & Sign Into Helium 10 Via: www.helium10.com.
- ○ Subscribe To Helium 10: Free 30 Day Trial Period.
- ○ Download & Install The Helium 10 Google Chrome Extension.
- ○ Select & Sign-Up For A Monthly Membership Plan For Helium 10.

Chapter 3:

Comprehensive Methods Of Conducting Product Discovery & Choosing Viable Profitable Merchandise To Retail On The Amazon Marketplace:

As an Amazon Seller you will be required to decide what type of merchandise you want to retail on the Amazon Marketplace through a process known as product discovery. Choosing what to sell and conducting the proper research can be a bit confusing, daunting, and challenging for some Amazon Sellers new to this process. To alleviate the stressfulness often associated with product discovery and due to the denseness of this subject I have broken this chapter down into (6) sections. These sections will provide you with a comprehensive understanding of the topic and an easy to follow outlined formula of tasks that you can utilize to locate viable profitable products to sell that fit your company's specific retail style.

Section #1:

(3) Product Options:

Option #1:

Some Amazon Sellers have ideas for an entirely new product therefore they opt to invent it from scratch.

The Process Of Inventing A Product From Scratch & Having It Manufactured Entails:

- o Choose The Type Of Product You Want To Invent.
- o Choose The Material You Require The Product To Made From (Rubber, Plastic, Metal, Wood, Etc.)
- o Choose The Dimension You Require The Product To Be.
- o Choose The Color You Require The Product To Be.
- o Draw An Illustration/Blueprint Of The Product That Includes All Specs & Features You Require Through The Use Of A 3D (CAD) Computer Aided Design Software Application, Such As SketchUp.
- o Design Your Primary Company Name, Brand Name, & Brand Logo Through The Use Of A Vector Based Graphics Computer Software Application, Such As Adobe Illustrator.
- o Have A Prototype Of Your Product Manufactured.

- Research & Locate A Reputable Supplier Through A (B2B) Marketplace Platform, Such As Alibaba To Manufacture A Mass Order Of The Product For You.
- Send Your SketchUp & Adobe Illustrator Art Files To Your Supplier.

*Note: You can create a free account, subscribe, install, download, and learn SketchUp for your (PC) or (Mac) via the Google Chrome Web Browser at: www.sketchup.com

Pricing Schedule For SketchUp:

SketchUp Basic	SketchUp Shop	SketchUp Pro	SketchUp Studio
Free	$119/Annually	$299/Annually	$1199/Annually

Although the SketchUp Basic plan is offered free of charge it only allows users access to a minimal set of tools and limited admission to the software application therefore I recommend inventors to subscribe to the SketchUp Shop plan which provides users full access to the suite of 3D software tools necessary for product design.

*Note: If Option #1 will be your approach to locating a product, if they exist, I recommend conducting ample research into third-party sellers who list similar products so that you can first determine if there is a market for your invention and it will be profitable to retail. Furthermore, it is not a recommended option for Amazon Sellers new to the business that have a limited budget due to the initial startup costs associated with the process.

Option #2:

If you are not the inventor or the manufacturer of the products you will be retailing on the Amazon Marketplace, you can utilize a technique known as (PL) Private Labeling. This process entails locating a supplier to manufacture a pre-invented product with your primary company name, brand name, and brand logo printed on it.

The Process Of (PL) Private Labeling A Product & Having It Manufactured Entails:

- Choose The Type Of Product You Want To Private Label.
- Choose The Product Variations You Require.
- Design Your Primary Company Name, Brand Name, & Brand Logo Through The Use Of A Vector Based Graphics Computer Software Application, Such As Adobe Illustrator.
- Research & Locate A Reputable Supplier Through A (B2B) Marketplace Platform, Such As Alibaba To Manufacture A Mass Order Of The Product For You.

○ Send Your Adobe Illustrator Art Files To Your Supplier.

Option #3:

You can opt to reinvent/redesign an already existing product by differentiating it. You can manufacture a higher quality better developed option for customers to purchase than that of what your competitors are currently retailing on Amazon:

- Making the product easier for the customer to use, such as adding a handle to it for carrying purposes or having the merchandise come with a case utilized specifically for storage and travel purposes.

- Changing the materials used to manufacture the product thus making it unbendable or less breakable than your competitors.

- Changing the products overall design or dimensions, such as its shape, overall size, or thickness to make it easier to use, carry, and store.

- Adding new features to the product, such as adding a smartphone/tablet pocket to a backpack that simultaneously acts as a charging station by having a rechargeable battery pack port for the devices to plug into while the consumer is traveling.

- Adding additional functionality to the product, such as a making a backpack simultaneously a lunch box by adding a pocket designed to carry food that contains a re-freezable ice pack that can be inserted and taken out as needed.

- Have your product manufactured in more color variations in contrast to your competitor's offerings.

- Add artwork or a small printed interesting graphic or symbolic piece of artwork to the surface of the product that relates to the item itself, such as adding an intricately designed Mandala printed directly on the surface of a yoga mat.

Pro Tip: One manner in which you can locate products to reinvent/redesign is by researching competitor's product listings on Amazon that have high net sales revenue but a lower star rating and several negative reviews. You will then read through the customer reviews of these particular competitor's product listings in search of changes, added features, or functionality attributes that the consumer wished the particular type of merchandise had. You would then make the necessary changes to the product when having it manufactured thus reinventing/redesigning an already existing product and making it a more functionally viable option for the consumer to use.

The Process Of Reinventing/Redesigning A Product & Having It Manufactured Entails:

- Research Your Competitor's Product Listings & A Product You Want To Reinvent.
- Choose The Material You Require The Product To Comprised Of (Rubber, Plastic, Metal, Wood, Etc.)
- Choose The Dimension You Require The Product To Be.
- Choose The Color You Require The Product To Be.
- Draw An Illustration/Blueprint Of The Product That Includes All Specs & Features You Require Through The Use Of A 3D (CAD) Computer Aided Design Software Application, Such As SketchUp.
- Design Your Primary Company Name, Brand Name, & Brand Logo Through The Use Of A Vector Based Graphics Computer Software Application, Such As Adobe Illustrator.
- Research & Locate A Reputable Supplier Through A (B2B) Marketplace Platform, Such As Alibaba To Manufacture A Mass Order Of The Product For You.
- Send Your SketchUp & Adobe Illustrator Art Files To Your Supplier.

Section #2:

Product Discovery Methods

Where You Can Locate Product Ideas

Method #1: Aggressively spend time researching merchandise that is currently being sold on Amazon. As you search www.amazon.com I recommend utilizing Helium 10's suite of Amazon Seller statistical data tools in order to identify if the merchandise would be profitable for you to retail.

amazon

Amazon: Browse their merchandise remotely through their smartphone app or via: www.amazon.com

Pro Tips To Utilize When Conducting Product Discovery On Amazon:

1) Utilize the categories and subcategories sections in contrast to solely utilizing the search bar to conduct your product discovery.

2) Amazon typically makes recommendations for additional and alternative types of merchandise to purchase from within particular sections of each seller's product listings. These sections can be utilized by Amazon Sellers to locate a viable profitable product to

, as you individually research other seller's product listings be sure to wing sections commonly located within each seller's product listings.

Look For & Examine The Following Sections:

✓ Frequently bought together

✓ Sponsored products related to this item

✓ What other items do customers buy after viewing this item?

✓ Compare items

✓ Sponsored products related to this item

✓ Customers also shopped for

✓ **Popular products inspired by this item**

3) When you locate top sellers of a particular product I recommend navigating to their Amazon Storefront to examine the other merchandise they retail.

4) Although the level of competition tends to be fierce within the following categories and subcategory sections you can opt to utilize Amazon's daily updated movers-and-shakers, most-wished-for, new-releases, and best-sellers webpages at:

- www.amazon.com/gp/movers-and-shakers/
- www.amazon.com/gp/most-wished-for/
- www.amazon.com/gp/new-releases/
- www.amazon.com/Best-Sellers/zgbs/

*Note:

Technique For Utilizing Amazon's Best Sellers List To Conduct Product Discovery:

You can utilize the hyperlink provided above to navigate to Amazon's Best Sellers list which is a webpage that contains Amazon's most popular products based on sales volume. The information provided on these pages is revised on an hourly basis therefore the data is up-to-date and accurate. From Amazon's Best Seller's page you can navigate to different categories and subcategories where you can view the top (100) best-selling products within those categories which gives you ample product options. Although, I do not recommend simply choosing to retail a product directly from the Best Sellers list due to the typical competitiveness and saturation on the market, there is a way in which these pages can be useful for conducting product discovery.

Ultimately, If you are in search of a profitable product to retail I recommend choosing a category you are interested in from Amazon's Best Sellers page. You will then choose a product that piques your interest from the top (100) on any given category page you choose. You will then locate the specific seller of that merchandise. Click on their seller display name which will navigate you to their Amazon Storefront so that you can view all of the products they retail on the Amazon Marketplace. This is the place where you may be able to locate a viable profitable product to retail.

*Although, I have provided you with this advice, be sure to always conduct the proper comprehensive product research utilizing Helium 10 or another type of Amazon Seller software before forging ahead with any options you locate in this manner.

Method #2: Aggressively spend time researching merchandise in brick & mortar stores as well as on online within various e-commerce marketplace platforms and social media sites. When you locate a group of potential products you want to sell I recommend utilizing Helium 10's suite of Amazon Seller statistical data tools to cross reference it with www.amazon.com in order to identify if the merchandise would be profitable for you to retail.

E-commerce Platforms, Social Media Sites, & Brick & Mortar Locations To Utilize For Product Discovery:

*Note: To quickly and easily view any of the websites listed below refer to the Google Chrome Web Browser or download their mobile app via the Google Play Store (Android) or Apple App Store (iPhone).

Etsy: Product ideas may come from browsing seller's handmade items on the e-commerce platform: www.etsy.com

Pinterest: Product ideas may come from browsing images on the social media image and idea sharing platform: www.pinterest.com

Target: Browse their merchandise in their brick and mortar locations and remotely via: www.target.com

SHARPER IMAGE

Sharper Image: Browse their merchandise remotely via: www.sharperimage.com

Home Shopping Network: Watch the channel on TV and browse their merchandise remotely
via: www.hsn.com

FiNGERHUT

Fingerhut: Browse their merchandise remotely via: www.fingerhut.com and/or order their free catalogue from their website and receive it via mail.

jet

Jet: Browse their merchandise remotely via: https://jet.com

HOBBY LOBBY
Super Savings, Super Selection!

Hobby Lobby: Browse their merchandise in their brick and mortar locations and remotely via: www.hobbylobby.com

Walmart

Walmart: Browse their merchandise in their brick and mortar locations and remotely via: www.walmart.com

sears

Sears: Browse their merchandise remotely via: www.sears.com

wayfair

Wayfair: Browse their merchandise remotely via: www.wayfair.com

Sky Mall

Sky Mall: Browse their merchandise remotely via: https://skymall.com

Home Depot: Browse their merchandise in their brick and mortar locations and remotely via: www.homedepot.com

Canopy

Canopy: Browse their merchandise remotely via: www.canopy.co

KICKSTARTER

Kickstarter: Product ideas may come from browsing inventor's new concepts on the crowdfunding social media creativity and design platforms, such as: www.kickstarter.com or www.indiegogo.com

By no means am I suggesting that you try to copy inventions from a website, such as Kickstarter or Indiegogo, but utilization of this technique can help you discover new market trends & may even spark a completely fresh idea for a product you could retail on Amazon. Furthermore, you may discover that you could change the overall design of the merchandise you locate, excel its functionality in some manner, and add specific features to the product to make it better than what is currently being offered.

*Note: Please keep in mind, that although there is a specific method to doing so, if you have an inventive idea for a new product you can set up your own Kickstarter or Indiegogo account and attempt to receive crowdfunding for your project.

AliExpress

AliExpress: Browse supplier's merchandise remotely via: www.aliexpress.com

Alibaba.com
Global trade starts here

Alibaba: Browse supplier's merchandise remotely on the (B2B) Marketplace platform Alibaba.

Method #3:

f

Facebook Groups: If you do not already have one, I recommend creating a social media account on www.facebook.com. You will then research and join what are known as Facebook groups that pertain to your interests or are centered around the interest of a particular subject. By joining a defined Facebook group, you will gain access to the daily posts pertaining to the subject that group is centered on. You will then pay attention to the discussions within the groups daily posts which can potentially lead to learning what products the individuals from the group use or need ultimately assisting you locating profitable products to retail.

Facebook Group Product Example: By joining and examining the discussions taking place within a Facebook group focused on the topic of bicycling I learned that small messenger bags for cyclers are in high demand but that the product lacks a smartphone/tablet carrying pocket that simultaneously acts as a charging station by having a rechargeable battery pack port for the devices to plug into while the consumer is on-the-go. Therefore, I have learned that a messenger bag created for cyclists in mind that has the added pocket for a smartphone/tablet that contains a charger port is a potential product I could retail on Amazon.

When you locate a group of potential product ideas utilizing the Facebook Group method I recommend using Helium 10's suite of Amazon Seller statistical data tools to cross reference the products with www.amazon.com in order to identify if the merchandise would be profitable for you to retail.

Method #4: Utilize Helium 10's product discovery tool Black Box as was discussed within Chapter 2. When you locate a group of potential product ideas utilizing Black Box I recommend using Helium 10's suite of Amazon Seller statistical data tools to cross reference the products with www.amazon.com in order to identify if the merchandise would be profitable for you to retail.

Method #5: Look around your home and analyze your own habits while thinking of questions like:

- o What product do you use the most often?
- o What do you wish was a product that you owned and would make ample use of?
- o What products do you use that cause recurring purchases, such as the Airwick refillable plugins?
- o Is there an invention of a useful product that does not exist, but you wish you owned?
- o Is there a product that you use that would be better and more functional if it had an extra added feature? You could easily make the changes to the product and have it manufactured with these added features thus reinventing an already existing product.

*When you locate a group of potential product ideas utilizing Method #5 I recommend using Helium 10's suite of Amazon Seller statistical data tools to cross reference the products with www.amazon.com in order to identify if the merchandise would be profitable for you to retail.

Method #6: Numerous individuals come up with clever ways to make daily tasks easier to perform by creating home-made products or remedies known as life hacks. By researching life hack websites, watching YouTube videos relating to the topic, and browsing the information provided via smartphone apps available you may discover a profitable product idea that could be invented and retailed on Amazon.

Life Hack Product Example: By examining the life hacks located on the Android smartphone app listed below I found out that a coffee filter filled with silica will absorb moisture which can help control the humidity in enclosed areas, such as a closet. Therefore, from that information I came up with a product to retail that is a simple mesh bag filled with silica that can easily hang or simply be placed in any enclosed area to help keep moisture and mildew out of the space.

To Locate Life Hack Websites:

Perform a search on the Google Chrome Web Browser for "Life Hacks" to generate a list of numerous life hack websites, lists, tips, and tricks.

To Locate Life Hack Videos On YouTube, follow the instructional steps included with the labeled images below:

Step #1: Launch the Google Chrome Web Browser.

Step #2: Using your mouse, left-click and release on the Google "Apps" icon located at the top left-hand side of the Google Chrome Web Browser to launch the navigational software application window:

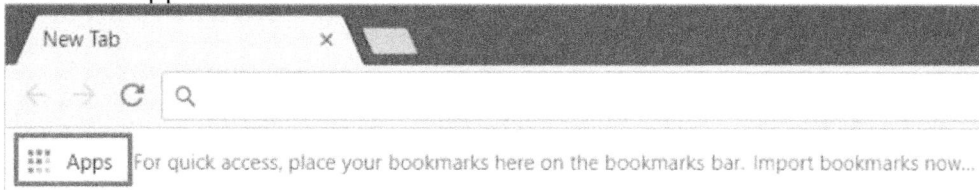

Step #3: Using your mouse, left-click and release on the YouTube launch button to be navigated directly to their web page:

Step #4: Enter the words "Life Hack" into the provided YouTube search bar which will generate a massive list of various videos related to the topic:

Life Hacks	Q

Life Hack Apps:

Life Hacks: Downloaded free of charge for Android devices from the Google Play Store.

Life Hacks: Downloaded for a one-time purchase charge of $1.99 for iPhones or iPads from the Apple App Store.

Method #7: Attend product trade shows to discover new merchandise and connect with suppliers in your country of residence or in foreign countries, such as the Canton Fair in China.

For A Comprehensive International Trade Fair Schedule & Description Of Each Type Held Refer To:

TradeFairDates: www.tradefairdates.com

Canton Fair: Is a tri-annually occurring internationally attended product trade show held in Guangzhou Pazhou, China that showcases hundreds of thousands of products and directly connects retailers with the suppliers of those goods.

Method #8: If you watch television, read magazines, browse the newspaper, spend time on social media sites, or shop in brick and mortar stores pay close attention to the products being advertised within those mediums or locations. Furthermore, if you are out running errands take notice of what products you observe others utilizing in their daily lives or purchasing at the stores you shop at. Be sure to take notes on your smartphone OneNote app that you downloaded in Chapter 3 or carry a notebook with you so that when you recognize a viable profitable product option for your company you can quickly jot it down and comprehensively research it on Amazon at a later time.

Fun Tip: Watch the ABC's famed television show "Shark Tank" and learn about new product inventions and the process the craft entails.

Section #3:

Various Recommendations & Helpful Hints To Utilize When Conducting Product Discovery:

Recommendations:

1) Although it may not always be the case due to lack of profitability I recommend retailing products that you understand, know how to use, and are passionate about. Think about your hobbies and then identify specific products that you would prefer to own in relation to your interests. Ultimately, understanding, knowing how to use, and being passionate about the products you are retailing will make the tasks of sourcing the item, building your Amazon product listings, and marketing the merchandise much easier to perform. Furthermore, you can opt to discuss your friends and family's hobbies with them and identify the products they are passionate about or may have a use for.

2) Do not put too much strain on solely searching for products you, your friends, or family are passionate about. As long a product is selling well on Amazon, it has low competition, and is profitable for you to retail, you can order a sample from your supplier to understand its use and comprehensively research its attributes online thus getting to know the product in-depth. Ultimately, you will not always have a personal use for some of the items that you locate while conducting product discovery but that does not mean that other individuals feel the same way.

3) Instead of attempting to research numerous products from various categories thus making your product discovery broad I recommend narrowing your product search parameters down by choosing one or two particular categories or subcategories that you want to focus on retailing in. You will then search products only relating to those particular categories thus alleviating the confusion that can result from attempting to search for merchandise within all categories ultimately identifying a target market of consumers.

4) You may opt to focus on locating a particular niche market and retailing products relating to the specific function of that niche.

Niche Market Example:

For example, per se, you were interested in retailing rock climbing gear, but you broke it down to the niche market of ice rock climbing gear and you sold products used to traverse ice covered rocks and camp in sub-below climates.

5) One way of conducting product discovery is to choose to focus on researching solely standard-sized or oversized products which narrows your search parameters down to merchandise matching one tier size or the other. There are disadvantages and benefits that should be taken into consideration when opting to retail products on the Amazon Marketplace that fit within one product tier size versus the other.

There are (2) pricing tiers known as:

(Standard-Size)
(Oversized)

*Note: For a precise definition of what qualifies as a standard-sized and oversized product according to Amazon's (TOS) Terms Of Service please refer to the next page for Amazon's (FBA) Fee Schedules.

Flat Rate Product Fulfillment Dimensions & Fee Schedules:

Standard-Size Product Unit:

❖ **Small Standard-Size:**

- Weight: **(1)** Lb. or less
- Dimensions: **(15x12x0.75)** Inches or less

❖ **Large Standard-Size**

- Weight: **(20)** Lbs. or less
- Dimensions: Between: **(15x12x0.75-18x14x8)** Inches

Product Dimensions & Weight	Flat Rate Product Fulfillment Fee Per Unit
Small Standard-Size: • 10 oz. or less • 15x12x0.75 inches or less	$2.50
Small Standard-Size: • 10-16 oz. • 15x12x0.75 inches or less	$2.63
Large Standard-Size: • 10 oz. or less • Between: 15x12x0.75-18x14x8 inches	$3.31
Large Standard-Size: • 10-16 oz. • Between: 15x12x0.75-18x14x8 inches	$3.48
Large Standard-Size: • 1-2 lbs. • Between: 15x12x0.75-18x14x8 inches	$4.90
Large Standard-Size: • 2-3 lbs. • Between: 15x12x0.75-18x14x8 inches	$5.42
Large Standard-Size: • 3-20 lbs. • Between: 15x12x0.75-18x14x8 inches	$5.42 + $0.38/lb. for each lb. over (3) lbs.

Oversized Product Unit:

- Weight: **(21)** Lbs. Or Greater
- Exceeds The Dimensions: **(18x14x8)** Inches

Product Dimensions & Weight	Flat Rate Product Fulfillment Fee Per Unit
Small Oversized: • Between: 0-71 lbs. • Between: 19x15x9-60x30 inches • Length + Girth must not exceed: 130 inches	$8.26 + $0.38/lb. for each lb. over (2) lbs.
Medium Oversized: • Weight must not exceed 151 lbs. • Longest side must not exceed: 108 inches • Length + Girth must not exceed: 130 inches	$11.37 + $0.39/lb. for each lb. over (2) lbs.
Large Oversized: • Weight must not exceed 151 lbs. • Longest side must not exceed: 108 inches • Length + Girth must not exceed 165 inches	$75.78 + $0.79/lb. for each lb. over 90 lbs.
Special Oversized: • Any unit over 150 lbs. • Longest side: Over 108 inches • Length + Girth: Over 165 inches	$137.32 + $0.91/lb. for each lb. above 90 lbs.

Standard-Sized Products:

Benefits:

- Standard-sized products typically have a lower shipping cost from your supplier to your location or to the Amazon Product Fulfillment Center in comparison to shipping oversized products.

- (FBA) fees for standard-sized products are lower than that of oversized products.

- Individually packaging standard-sized products typically costs less in comparison to oversized products.

- Branding standard-sized products typically costs less in comparison to oversized products due to the size of the logos needing to be printed.

Disadvantages:

- Storage fees per cubic foot are higher on standard-sized products in comparison to oversized products.

- Due to the benefits mentioned above Amazon is saturated with third-party sellers who solely sell standard-sized products thus causing fierce competition in several product categories which tends to make locating a profitable standard-sized product that resides in a non-competitive less saturated category a more difficult task for you as an Amazon Seller.

Oversized Products:

Benefits:

- Storage fees per cubic foot are lower on oversized products in comparison to standard-sized products.

- Many third-party sellers opt to stray away from selling oversized products due to the disadvantages listed below. What this means to you as an Amazon Seller is that if you opt to sell oversized products then you have the potential to enter a less saturated product category on Amazon with minimal competition from third-party sellers thus resulting in your ability to more easily locate a profitable product to retail and quickly rank to the top of page one of customer generated search results when you list the merchandise ultimately dominating sales in the particular product market you enter.

Disadvantages:

- Oversized products typically have a higher shipping cost from your supplier to your location or to the Amazon Product Fulfillment Center in comparison to shipping standard-sized products.

- (FBA) fees for oversized products are higher than that of standard-sized products.

- Individually packaging oversized products typically costs more in comparison to standard-sized products.

- Branding oversized products typically costs more in comparison to standard-sized products due to the size of the logos needing to be printed.

*Note: Although Amazon's monthly storage fee for third-party sellers partaking in the (FBA) program is cheaper per cubic foot on oversized merchandise in contrast to standard-sized the expense can still add up rather quickly. Therefore, if you are opting to sell oversized products through the (FBA) program pay close attention to the cubic foot dimensions of the merchandise you are researching to sell and be sure to calculate the monthly storage fee totals to be certain the items will still be profitable before moving forward with your decision.

6) One way of conducting product discovery is to choose a specific price tier to focus on researching, such as solely identifying merchandise that is retailing at a product price point of ($30) per unit which narrows your search down to goods matching that one price point tier or if you are opting to sell more expensive merchandise you can opt to research goods that are exclusively retailing at a product price point of ($75) per unit.

Pro Tip:

I would like to briefly discuss product price point range differences and their impact on competition levels on the Amazon Marketplace in association with researching new merchandise to retail.

Numerous third-party sellers on Amazon typically tend to gear towards retailing merchandise that is priced at ($20) or less because the initial entry level barrier to these product markets aka landing costs are considerably lower than that of goods that sell at, per se, ($30-$50) per unit. Although, the landing costs may be lower within these particular markets, they are generally oversaturated and highly competitive. Selling less expensive merchandise can lead to much lower profit margins due to the fact that increased competition levels can tend to result in higher (PPC) expenditure as well as less sales on account of over-saturation on the market depending on the category and niche you choose. Ultimately, if you instead opt to retail a bit more expensive/higher quality type of merchandise within the ($30, $50, or even $100) per unit product price point range you may have a lower per unit daily sales volume but there is much more opportunity for increased profit margins and success.

7) When conducting product research, you could attempt to focus on locating products that are primarily currently only being sold by shipment means of (FBM) aka (MFN) on Amazon. You could then be one of the few sellers that offers a similar product to customers as an (FBA) item which means that consumers would now have the ability to receive the item within (1-2) days shipping time in contrast to the typical (1-2) week shipping time that occurs with products sold by means of (MFN). By being one of the only Amazon Sellers that offers an item via (FBA) you have the opportunity to dominate the category you are selling the merchandise within due to the fact that customers tend to favor purchasing products from sellers that offer the shortest shipping time.

When utilizing this method of product discovery, I recommend investigating the first top (1-10) product listings on the first page of search results shown on Amazon for a specific type of merchandise within the subcategory it resides. If you determine that at least (5) out of the first (10) product listings are currently selling via (MFN) then you have a good chance of dominating the particular market you are researching by offering a similar product via (FBA).

A simple method to quickly evaluate if your top competitors on Amazon are retailing via (FBA) or (MFN) within any particular product category is through utilization of Helium 10's Amazon product research tool Xray.

To Determine Whether A Product Is Retailing Via (FBA) or (MFN), follow the instructional steps included with the labeled images below:

For the following example of determining whether merchandise is primarily retailing via (FBA) or (MFN) I will be utilizing a product known as "Home Brew Kits For Beer" currently selling on Amazon.

Step #1: Navigate to www.amazon.com from within the Google Chrome Web Browser and be sure to have Helium 10's Google Chrome Extension downloaded, installed, and prepared for use as was discussed in Chapter 2.

Step #2: Type the keywords "Home Brew Kits For Beer" into Amazon's search bar and perform a search for the product which will navigate you to a page containing the first (1-48) product listings pertaining to your keyword search entry:

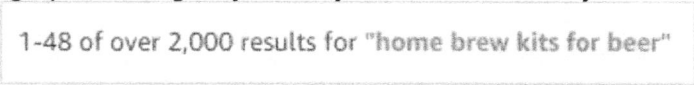

1-48 of over 2,000 results for "home brew kits for beer"

Step #3: Once you are navigated to the first page of Amazon product listings containing "Home Brew Kits For Beer" you will use your mouse to left-click and release on Helium 10's Google Chrome Extension located on the top right-hand side of the Google Chrome Web Browser which will generate a list of navigational task buttons:

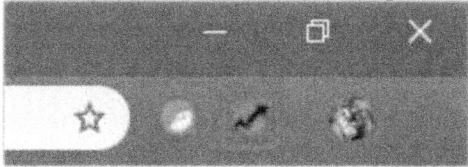

Step #4: Using your mouse, left-click and release on Helium 10's Amazon product research tool Xray which will enable the software to generate your competitions statistical seller data in relation to "Home Brew Kits For Beer":

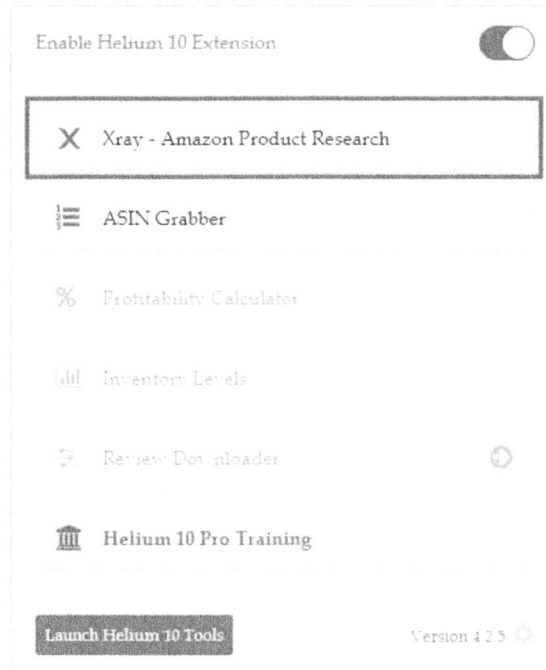

Enable Helium 10 Extension

X   Xray - Amazon Product Research

≣   ASIN Grabber

%   Profitability Calculator

᠁   Inventory Levels

⌕   Review Downloader

🏛   Helium 10 Pro Training

Launch Helium 10 Tools   Version 4.2.5

Step #5: As you can observe in the screenshot below, Helium 10's Amazon product research tool Xray has notified me that (5) of the top third-party competitors of "Home Brew Kits For Beer" retail the merchandise via (MFN) which means that there may be an opportunity to excel in sales and dominate this market by offering a similar product to consumers via (FBA):

Xray - Amazon Product Research - home brew kits for beer (search volume: 1,951)

Total Revenue	Avg. Revenue	Avg. BSR	Avg. Price	Avg. Reviews
$307,292	$6,538	77,512	$88.52	120

#	ASIN	Brand	Title	Category	BuyBox	#		Price
1	B0765CZ6P9	Northern ...	SP Northern Brewer - Brew. Share. ...	Kitchen & Dining	Northern Bre...	1	MFN	$109.99
2	B07J1YR7FS	Northern ...	SP Northern Brewer Deluxe Home...	Kitchen & Dining	Northern Bre...	1	MFN	$199.95
3	B07RYNRKY9	BrewDem...	SP BrewDemon Craft Beer Kit with ...	Kitchen & Dining	BadgerTracker	1	FBA	$89.00
4	B00IYNBV7Q	Craft A Br...	Craft A Brew Home Brewing Kit ...	Kitchen & Dining	Craft a Brew	9	FBA	$44.99
5	B001BCFUBU	Mr. Beer	Mr. Beer 2 Gallon Complete Star...	Kitchen & Dining	Amazon	2	AMZ	$43.90
6	B0179ZH89Y	Northern ...	Northern Brewer Brew. Share. E...	Kitchen & Dining	Northern Bre...	1	MFN	$109.99
7	B0178BWOIE	Northern ...	Northern Brewer Deluxe Home...	Kitchen & Dining	Northern Bre...	2	MFN	$199.95
8	B005G20IIG	Brooklyn ...	Brooklyn Brew Shop Everyday I...	Kitchen & Dining	Amazon	7	AMZ	$41.70
9	B00W3PXJ4Y	Northern ...	Northern Brewer - 1 Gallon Craf...	Kitchen & Dining	Northern Bre...	1	MFN	$49.99
10	B07L35H735	KLARSTEIN	Klarstein Mundschenk • 8 Gallo...	Kitchen & Dining	Berlin Brand...	1	FBA	$329.99

*Note: When it states (AMZ) as the product fulfillment method it means that the product is sold first-party by Amazon and is available to ship within (1-2) days.

Helpful Hints:

1) When choosing your first product I recommend opting for an item that allows you to expand your brand by retailing related merchandise within the same category that your first product resides. For example, per se, you chose to sell sleeping bags therefore you are retailing camping gear. If your first product is profitable I then recommend expanding your brand to include other camping related gear such as a, tent, sleeping mat, portable cookware kit, foldable multi-tool, lantern, headlamp, water resistant lighter, and so on.

Building A Solid Brand That Retails Relatable Products Is Beneficial For The Following Reasons:

- If you retail several types of products residing in separate Amazon categories you will more than likely necessitate a different (B2B) supplier for each type of merchandise you sell which can be a tedious time consuming task. If you instead opt to focus on one product category you will potentially be able to obtain relatable items from (1) supplier thus allowing you to devote more time and energy to properly exponentially expanding one brand. For example, a supplier on a (B2B) Marketplace platform, such as Alibaba may manufacture a camping cookware kit, but you may learn that they also produce numerous other camping related gear as well, which means they could become your sole supplier for these types of products. Ultimately, by developing one brand that sells relatable merchandise within one specific Amazon product category you can alleviate the tedious task of searching for, building relationships, and managing various orders from numerous suppliers which allows you to devote more time to product discovery, conducting ample product research, and proper product design.

- When you retail products that reside in the same category you create the opportunity to have Amazon recommend your other relatable products to the customer from within your product listings. For example, if you sell, per se, several related products, such as camping gear then Amazon will recognize this and when a customer is viewing one of your camping gear product listings then your other camping gear product listings will be recommended at the bottom of the current product listing in which they are viewing thus resulting in free advertising that leads customers to purchasing your other merchandise.

- If your ultimate goal is to sell the brand you create I highly encourage you to center its design around products that corelate within a specific category. Utilization of this tactic will result in your ability to gain prospective buyer's attention when the time comes to sell thus resulting in the eventual sale of your brand for a hefty sum.

2) You may want to research products to retail that require the consumer to incur repeat purchases to continue using the product thus helping you to obtain recurring sales by the same customers either weekly, monthly, or annually.

Recurring Sales Product Example:

As you can observe in the following images, Air Wick is a company that has significantly capitalized on retailing merchandise focused on consumer's being required to repeat purchases to continue utilizing their products. They currently retail an electric air freshener, which is a one-time purchase, but it requires a separately purchased scented liquid Air Wick cartridge to make it work that lasts approximately (4) weeks and then necessitates a replacement cartridge. Therefore, to continue utilizing the air freshener device the customer is required to purchase at least one cartridge per month thus resulting in monthly recurring purchases of this company's product.

Image: Air Wick's Electric Air Freshener:

Image: Air Wick's Plug-In Refill Cartridges:

3) Please be aware, that simplistic practical daily use merchandise has the potential to sell well, such as easy to manufacture safety work gloves located within the Tools & Home Improvement category, which means you do not have to focus solely on retailing fancy extravagant high-end merchandise, such as jewelry, watches, or smartphones to catch a buyer's attention and procure a large sales volume from your product listing. With that said, due to typical high-levels of third-party seller competition & over saturation on the market with simplistic goods, such as safety work gloves, I do not recommend entering such a category/subcategory unless you can somehow differentiate the product by adding a feature to it that makes the merchandise more functional for the consumer in contrast to the other seller's similar product offers. Ultimately, if (1000) third-party sellers are retailing the same exact type of product for a similar price and your offer is not distinguished in one way or another that provides added value for the customer then it will generally be difficult to procure sales in the category you are attempting to retail in. Furthermore, by simplistic I do not mean for you to search out, manufacture, and sell low-quality poorly made merchandise. What I am stating is that simplistic high-quality practical daily use items with an added feature have the ability to generate an extensive customer following, sales volume, and sizable profit margin depending on your ability to think outside the box so to speak when you are conducting product discovery. On a further note, as you can observe in the images below, occasionally a product idea with an added feature will result in you initially beginning your search within a simplistic subcategory, such as "Safety Work Gloves", which may lead you to a particular separate less competitive subcategory/niche market or at least provide you with an idea of how you could differentiate the merchandise as it has done for me when providing you with the following product examples.

Image #1: Simplistic Product Example With No Added Feature:

1) Fingerless Safety Work Gloves
2) Primary Category: Tools & Home Improvement
3) Subcategory: Safety Work Gloves
4) Highly Competitive
5) Overly Saturated On The Market

Image #2: Simplistic Product Example With Added Feature Located After Initially Researching The Subcategory "Safety Work Gloves" From Image #1:

1) Fingerless (LED) Flashlight Work Gloves
2) Primary Category: Tools & Home Improvement
3) Subcategory: Hands Free Flashlights
4) Less Competitive In Comparison To Image #1
5) Less Saturated On The Market In Comparison To Image #1
6) Added Feature/Differentiation=(LED) Lights

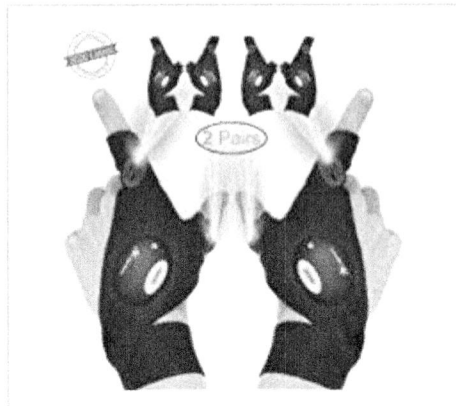

4) Instead of solely focusing on one product to sell you could identify a particular product category and research (2) or more related products that serve a similar purpose that can simultaneously be retailed together as an all-in-one kit aka bundling versus being sold separately. For example, instead of opting to sell one single pair of gardening shears you could opt to retail an all-in-one gardening tool kit that includes all of the essential equipment utilized in horticultural.

Image: Gardening Tool Kit:

5) One fact that you must understand when researching products to sell is that some types of merchandise are seasonal, which means they are only in demand and purchased by consumers during a particular part of the year in either the winter, spring, summer, or autumn months. These types of products have to do with an outdoor activity, the climate outside, sporting events, or a holiday celebration, which means they are only, for the most part, profitable to sell during the associated season the merchandise is utilized within. This is important to you as an Amazon Seller on account that if you opt to retail these types of products you must be financially prepared for a lull in sales during certain seasons which means you will not be incurring sales or making profit during those particular times of the year on your seasonally based Amazon product listings. Furthermore, you must pay close attention to inventory levels on seasonal products during your peak sale times, which means you must be well-stocked and prepared for a high influx of sales during the season your merchandise sells within. On the contrary, if you are opting for (FBA) as your product fulfillment method then you do not want to be overly stocked when your seasonal product is out of its peak sales season due to the long-term storage fees your merchandise will incur.

Seasonal Product Examples:

Winter:

- Insulated Cold Weather Apparel (Coats, Socks, Stocking Caps, Scarves, & Gloves)
- Fleece Pajamas
- Fleece Lined Boots
- Hand Warmers
- Ice Scraper
- Snowboarding Equipment

Spring:

- Gardening Tools & Accessories
- Spring Related Decorations & Artwork

Summer:

- Pool Toys
- Boating Gear & Accessories
- Sandals & Flip-Flops
- Men's & Women's Swimsuits
- Beverage Coolers & Drink Koozies

Autumn:

- Leaf Blower
- Disposable Leaf Bags
- Back-To-School Supplies & Accessories
- Pumpkin Scented Candles & Air Fresheners

Holiday Celebrational Seasonal Product Examples:

- Christmas Decorations & Accessories (Winter)
- Christmas & Thanksgiving Cookbooks (Autumn & Winter)
- Valentine's Day Related Gifts (Winter)
- St. Patrick's Day Gear (Winter)
- Easter Decorations & Related Gifts (Spring)
- Halloween Costumes & Decorations (Autumn)
- Thanksgiving Decorations & Accessories (Autumn)
-

Sporting Event Seasonal Product Examples:

- NHL Sports Gear (Autumn & Winter)
- NFL Sports Gear (Autumn)
- MLB Sports Gear (Spring & Summer)
- NBA Sports Gear (Autumn & Winter)

Seasonal Product Pro Tips:

Pro Tip #1: As you conduct product discovery you can utilize Helium 10's Google Chrome Extension Xray to research a particular products yearly sales history on Amazon which will help you to determine if the merchandise is a seasonally selling item. For example, as you can observe in the screenshot below, when examining the yearly sales history of a gardening tool kit I have determined that it primarily retails during the spring month of May ultimately making it a seasonal product.

Image: Yearly Product Sales History For A Gardening Tool Kit Product Listing With Emphasis On The Spring Sales Season:

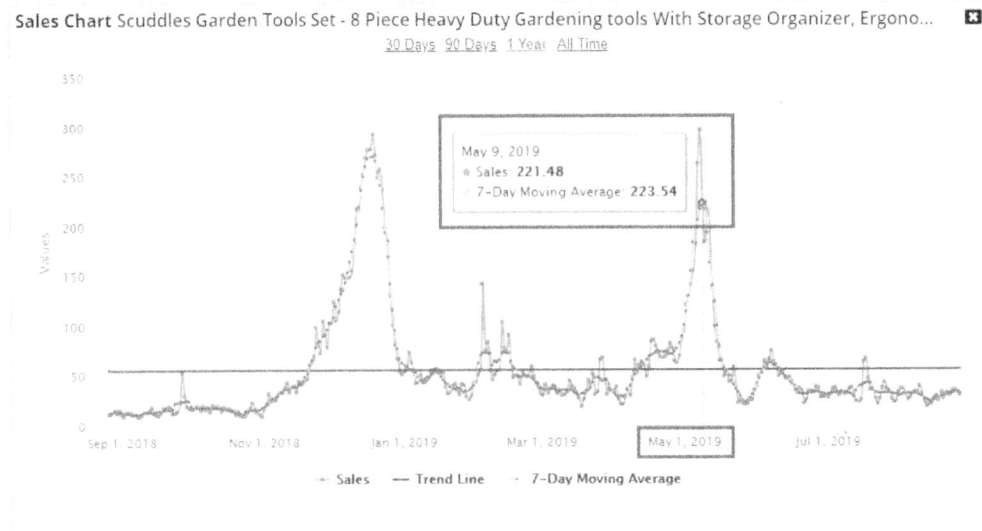

Sales Chart Scuddles Garden Tools Set - 8 Piece Heavy Duty Gardening tools With Storage Organizer, Ergono...
30 Days 90 Days 1 Year All Time

May 9, 2019
Sales 221.48
7-Day Moving Average 223.54

Sales — Trend Line — 7-Day Moving Average

Pro Tip #2: As you can observe in the screenshot below, some products may be bi-seasonal, such as the gardening tool kit which means that although it primarily retails during the spring months it also sees an influx in sales during the Christmas holiday season due to the fact that it makes for a great gift idea. Ultimately, if you are opting to sell a seasonal product it may be a good idea to choose a bi-seasonal type of merchandise that could appeal either to the consumer for their personal use throughout its peak sales season or given as a gift to their friends and loved ones during the holiday Christmas season.

Image: Yearly Product Sales History For A Gardening Tool Kit Product Listing With Emphasis On The Winter Sales Season:

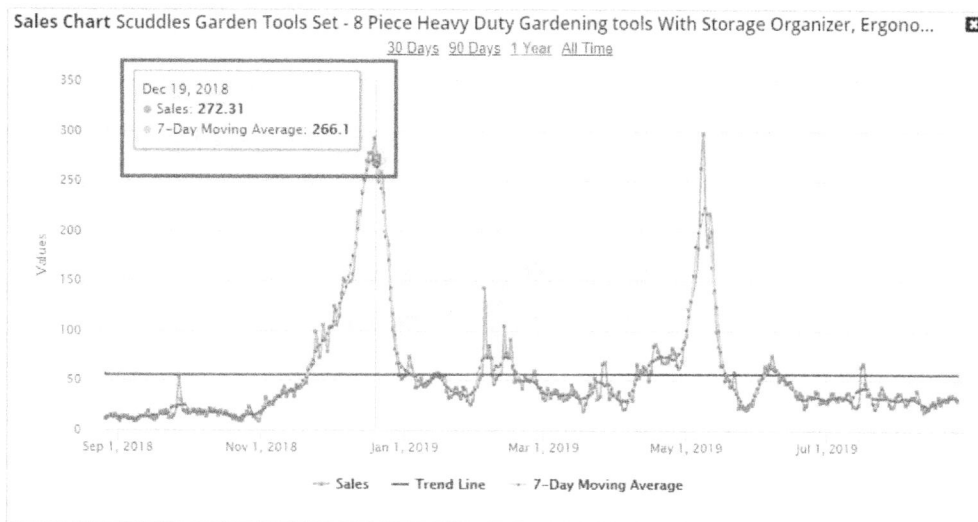

6) Amazon manufactures its own line of merchandise and retails it under the brand name Amazon Basics thus making them a first-party seller of several products on Amazon. As you conduct product discovery pay close attention to whether or not Amazon is one of the first-party sellers of the merchandise you are researching to retail. If Amazon is a first-party seller of the product in question I will warn you as a third-party seller it can tend to be difficult to compete with them.

It is Difficult To Compete With Amazon's First-Party Sales For The Following Reasons:

- Consumers may opt for Amazon's first-party products on account that they typically cost less than products being sold by third-party sellers.

- The consumer may opt to choose a product directly sold by Amazon titled Amazon Basics due to the fact that they trust Amazon in contrast to opting to purchase from a third-party seller that they are unfamiliar with.

- Since Amazon owns the brand this means that their massive marketing team internally builds, optimizes, manages, and advertises their Amazon Basic's product listings which ultimately makes it difficult for third-party sellers offering similar products to compete.

With those facts stated just because Amazon retails a product it does not mean that you cannot compete with them by selling something similar. Remember they will most likely only be one of the product listings among many on the page within the particular category you are researching which means that there is still a chance for customers to view and choose your product over that of Amazons. Ultimately, if you are opting to compete with Amazon's first-party sales I only recommend doing so if you can locate a supplier that can offer you a higher quality better developed version of a similar product than what Amazon is currently retailing. You will then have to be certain that you can get the merchandise manufactured for a reasonable cost in order to competitively price your product listing against that of Amazon's offer.

To view all products manufactured by Amazon retailed under the brand name Amazon Basics navigate via the Google Chrome Web Browser to: www.amazon.com/amazonbasics

7) As you research products to retail I recommend recording your findings in an organized list and saving them via computer into a word document. This will allow you to easily evaluate your findings, determine profitability, and ultimately compare each product before making your final decision of what to source and retail on the Amazon Marketplace.

Record:

- The name of the company that currently retails the product.
- The brand name of the product.
- The location you found the product.
- An image of the product.
- Dimensions of the product.
- Any related product data, such as price, size variations, color variations, its features, its functionality, and the materials used to manufacture the product.
- Any customer reviews you may find that state information in regard to changes the consumer wished the product had, such as added features or more functionality.

Section #4:

Perform The Proper Cautionary Steps To Ensure A Pleasant & Safe Experience For The Customer When Retailing The Following Types Of Products On The Amazon Marketplace:

1) Products That Require Assembly By The Customer Upon Receival:

If you opt to retail a product that requires assembly by the customer upon receival than you must make sure that the process of assembling the product is simple and easy for consumers to perform. If the assembly process is too complex then you may experience a large volume of negative customer reviews for your product listing, low star ratings, and an influx of returned units. A large number of bad reviews and product returns can have a negative impact on your Amazon Seller performance metrics which can be harmful to your reputation on the Amazon Marketplace and monetarily damaging for your company. Therefore, when you opt to retail a product that requires assembly upon receival, I recommend being absolutely certain that all of the necessary parts are present in each order and that the pieces are stored in easy-to-read labeled polybags. Furthermore, your product packaging must also contain an easily understandable comprehensive well-written step-by-step instruction manual with text accompanied by images that explains how to perform the product assembly process.

2) Electronic Products:

Electronic products are highly vulnerable to incurring damage during the shipping process from your supplier to your location due to climatic changes involving humidity, cold, and heat. Furthermore, the shipping boxes and containers that your electronics are being transported in may incur constant vibrations and hard impacts which can also harm electronic products. Therefore, if you are going to be retailing electronic products, before selling the merchandise to your consumers, upon receival of a mass order from your supplier I recommend personally inspecting each unit by plugging it in or turning it on to be sure that the product is properly functioning.

4) Products Made For Use By Infants, Toddlers, & Children:

When you are retailing products made for use by infants, toddlers, and young children I recommend that you properly label both the product itself and its individual product packaging with a choking hazard warning when applicable to protect the customers using your product as well as legally protect your company from an unnecessary consumer lawsuit. Furthermore, due to infants, toddlers, and young children having allergies you will want to know exactly what materials your products are comprised of and have them correctly labeled in detail on your individual product packaging to prevent an allergic reaction when the product is used by the consumer. Ultimately, when you sell products made for use by infants, toddlers, and young children you are required by law to have a (CPC) Children's Product Certificate, which can be drafted by you or your manufacturer. The information in a (CPC) can only be based on product test results from a (CPSC) Consumer Product Safety Commission accepted laboratory.

- To learn more about the topic and process (CPC) and (CPSC) children product testing entails please refer to: www.cpsc.gov

*Note: When you opt to retail products made for use by infants, toddlers, and young children I recommend acquiring Business Liability Insurance which financially protects your company's assets in the event of a formal consumer lawsuit.

3) Fragile Items:

If you are opting to retail fragile easily breakable products I recommend packaging the merchandise in sturdy durable high-quality protective packaging to prevent damage to the product during the shipment process. If products are commonly broken upon receival by your consumers then you may experience a large volume of negative customer reviews for your product listing, low star ratings, and an influx of returned units. I will reiterate the fact that a large number of bad reviews and product returns can have a negative impact on your Amazon Seller performance metrics which can be harmful to your reputation on the Amazon Marketplace and monetarily damaging for your company.

4) Products That Have A Sharp Edge Or The Ability To Cause An Accidental Injury:

If you are opting to retail products that have a sharp edge, such as a cooking knife set, be sure to properly label the product packaging with a warning label to prevent or dissuade consumers from attempting to sue your company in a court of law if the they injure themselves while using your merchandise.

*Note: When you opt to retail products that naturally have a sharp edge, such as a knife set, I recommend acquiring Business Liability Insurance which financially protects your company's assets in the event of a formal consumer lawsuit.

6) Vitamins, Dietary Supplements, Edibles, Body Care, Skin Care, Dermatological, & Cosmetic Products:

Although, these types of products can be profitable due to the fact that they are consumable which will cause recurring sales by the customer, to avoid a potential lawsuit from a customer there are product safety precautions that I recommend taking when opting to retail merchandise that is ingested or applied to the skin. These product safety precautions include properly labeling the product with a complete ingredient list and any allergy warnings. Furthermore, when applicable I suggest having the product tested and approved for human use or consumption by a certified lab. You will then use your certified lab results to have the merchandise approved by the (FDA) Food & Drug Administration (USA Only).

*Note: When you opt to retail products that are either ingested or applied to the skin I recommend acquiring Business Liability Insurance which financially protects your company's assets in the event of a formal consumer lawsuit.

Section #5:

The Importance Of Understanding Patent Ownership Rights:

I recommend legally protecting your company from getting sued for patent infringement by making it a general practice of investigating in your country of residence and those you intend on doing business within to see if anyone owns the rights to the particular design of a product before moving forward with manufacturing of your invention, redesign/reinvention, or private label product ideas. If your search generates (0) results from any of the vast intellectual property right's government databases listed below then there is no patent on the product design owned in regard to the merchandise you are researching. Furthermore, although I do not claim to be an expert on patent infringement, if a you find that a company does federally own the patent rights to the particular design of a product, I believe that it is legal to have a similar product that serves the same function manufactured as long as you change the overall design of the product.

(2) Methods For Performing A Patent Search:

Method #1: Research your competition and look for patent serial numbers typically printed on the product, its individual product packaging, or on the company's website for example (U.S. Patent No. 7,555,879). You will then input the patent serial numbers you locate into the patent search online databases at the official intellectual property government operated database websites listed below.

Method #2: Another method of performing a patent search involves creating a list of keywords and keyword phrases related to the type of product or technology you are researching. You will then input the keywords and keyword phrases related to the product you are investigating into the patent search online databases at the official intellectual property government operated database websites listed on the following page.

You Can Perform A Search For Patent Ownership At The Following Official Intellectual Property Government Operated Database Websites:

Country	Official Intellectual Property Website
United States	www.uspto.gov
Canada	www.ic.gc.ca
Australia	www.ipaustralia.gov.au
United Kingdom	www.gov.uk

*Note: If you reside in or are attempting to search for ownership of a patent within a different country than one of the (4) listed above you can locate the country's official intellectual property government website by conducting an Internet search.

How To Apply For & Obtain A Federally Registered Patent For Your Product Design:

Although it is not required by law to obtain a patent for your product design, if you want to legally protect your invention or design from being replicated and sold by another company I recommend applying for, purchasing, and obtaining a federally registered patent in your country of residence as well as those that you intend on doing business within.

(2) Types Of Patents You Can File:

1) **Utility Patent:** Is patent given to an individual who invents or discovers any new and useful process, a machine, or any beneficial improvement to an already existing product.

An example of a utility patent would be, per se, you took a regular dog collar, but you added LED lights to the collar so that it lights up at night in order for the owner to safely walk their dog in the dark without the fear of traffic not seeing them. You could file for a utility patent on that design since you made a beneficial improvement to an already existing product.

2) **Design Patent:** Is a patent given to an individual who invents a new ornamental design of a product or essentially redesigns an already existing product. Per se, as an Amazon Seller you change the overall design of a private label product and your layout is not yet patented you could then file for a design patent on the idea you created.

An Example Of A Company That Filed A Design Patent Is Crocs:

You Can Apply For, Pay For, & Obtain A Federally Registered Patent At The Following Official Intellectual Property Government Operated Websites:

Country	Official Intellectual Property Website
United States	www.uspto.gov
Canada	www.ic.gc.ca
Australia	www.ipaustralia.gov.au
United Kingdom	www.gov.uk

*Note: If you reside in or are attempting to receive a federally registered patent from a different country than one of the (4) listed above you can locate the country's official intellectual property government website by conducting an Internet search.

To be absolutely certain you will not encounter any legal issues I recommend researching, locating, and hiring a patent attorney. If you do not have a personal attorney you can find numerous patent attorneys online that will help guide you through the complexities associated with the patent process. Simply enter patent attorney into the Google Chrome Web Browser search bar and it will give you various options or you can navigate to www.legalzoom.com. An attorney will be able to better answer any questions you may have in regard to acquiring a legally registered patent for your product design and they will also be able to conduct extensive formal research for you.

Before moving forward with applying for your legally registered federally protected patent I recommend reading through the vast amount of literature and watching the how to videos associated with the patent process provided by the official intellectual property government operated websites listed above.

Section #6:

Statistical Data Analysis Techniques To Utilize When Conducting Product Discovery On Amazon:

Once you identify a potential product to retail or several, before moving forward with your decision to manufacture the merchandise, I recommend utilizing Amazon in accordance with Helium 10's suite of software tools to comprehensively investigate the product's statistical listing data to determine its success score, level of third-party seller competition, (BSR), popularity among customers, projected per unit sales, and profitability margins.

Your ultimate goal when conducting product discovery and performing statistical data analysis should focus on locating merchandise that has a mid to high success score, a low (BSR), a sizeable volume of monthly keyword search among customers, a healthy constant amount of daily/yearly unit sales, and retrieves no less than a (30%) gross profitability gain per unit.

An important subject you must comprehend before delving into the following lesson on statistical data analysis is the ideology that customers purchasing merchandise on Amazon typically tend to buy items that are located somewhere on the first page of keyword specific generated product listings results. Essentially, a customer will perform a search for a product utilizing specific keywords entered into Amazon's search bar that are related to the goods they intend to purchase. The consumers keyword search will then generate all of the product listings on Amazon that pertain to the type of merchandise in accordance to their keyword search for the goods they are attempting to locate. If a customer is utilizing a computer to perform a search for a product Amazon tends to generate approximately (24-48) product listings results per page. On the contrary, if a customer is utilizing their smartphone or tablet to perform a search for a product Amazon tends to generate approximately (16-24) product listings results per page. The customer is then required to click the gray "Next" navigational button if they would like to view the subsequent page of product listings related to their specific keyword search. What this means to you as an Amazon Seller, is that the closer your product listing is to the number one spot on the first page of generated (1-16), (1-24), or (1-48) keyword specific product listing results the better chance you have to procure sales and dominate the subcategory you are retailing in. What you do not want is to be the last product listing located on the last page of generated search results. If the latter was the case, then most customers would never see your product listing and procuring sales would be extremely unlikely. Therefore, your goal for each product you list is to attempt to become the first product listing on the first page that a customer views when they perform a keyword search for a specific product or to at least have your product listing located somewhere on the first page of generated keyword specific results. The importance of this topic in regard to statistical data analysis is the philosophy that if you research at least the top (1-16) of your competitors' product listings located on the first page of generated keyword specific results you can acquire an approximate idea of whether the specific merchandise you are investigating will be profitable for you to retail and whether or not you could succeed entering the specific market you are investigating. Therefore, for the remainder of the lessons in this section I will be focusing on illustrating how to perform statistical data analysis by examining the top (1-16) competitors' product listings in relation to one specific type of merchandise, keyword phrase and subcategory.

For the following (18) lessons on statistical data analysis I will be utilizing a product known as a "Baby Sling" currently selling on Amazon.

Image: Baby Sling:

1) Baby Sling
2) Primary Category: Baby
3) Subcategory: Child Carrier Slings
4) Primary Keyword Phrase: Baby Sling

First Step In Conducting Statistical Data Analysis:

Through the utilization of the research tool Xray, Helium 10 provides their users with something known as a star rating system which is a quick overview score of a products likelihood of success on Amazon for a third-party seller investigating a new market to enter. Although, Helium 10's success score does not provide comprehensive data for you to evaluate it is based on information, such as your competitors' customer star rating levels, review count, and sales distribution among the sellers already dominating the specific keyword phrase or subcategory you are researching. It can assist you in predetermining the level of third-party seller competition, quality of the products already in the specific keyword phrase or subcategory you are investigating, and the maturity of the market. Ultimately, the success score can be utilized as a quick way for you to screen a keyword phrase or subcategory to determine if it is worth your time to continue investigating. Therefore, the first step in statistical data analysis is to determine Helium 10's success score star rating value of the specific keyword phrase or subcategory you are researching.

How The Star Rating Values Operate:

(1) Star: A subcategory or keyword phrase with a success score of (1) is not worth your time to continue investigating.

(1.5) Star: A subcategory or keyword phrase with a success score of (1.5) stars is typically not worth your time to continue investigating but do not always pass these product options up without some initial evaluation.

(2) Stars: A subcategory or keyword phrase with a success score of (2) stars or above is worth your time to continue investigating.

(3) Stars: A subcategory or keyword phrase with a success score of (3) stars or above is definitely worth your time to continue investigating.

(4) Stars: A subcategory or keyword phrase with a success score of (4) stars or above is rare and would certainly be worth your time to continue investigating.

(5) Stars: A subcategory or keyword phrase with a success score of (5) is extremely rare and would unquestionably be worth your time to continue investigating.

To Determine The Star Rating Success Score Of A Product, follow the instructional steps included with the labeled images below:

Step #1: Navigate to www.amazon.com from within the Google Chrome Web Browser and be sure to have Helium 10's Google Chrome Extension downloaded, installed, and prepared for use as was discussed in Chapter 2.

Step #2: Type the keywords "Baby Sling" into Amazon's search bar and perform a search for the product which will navigate you to a page containing the first (1-48) product listings pertaining to your keyword phrase search entry:

1-48 of 925 results for "baby sling"

Step #3: Once you are navigated to the first page of Amazon product listings containing baby slings you will use your mouse to left-click and release on Helium 10's Google Chrome Extension located on the top right-hand side of the Google Chrome Web Browser which will generate a list of navigational task buttons:

Step #4: Using your mouse, left-click and release on Helium 10's Amazon product research tool Xray which will enable the software to generate your competitions statistical seller data in relation to "Baby Sling":

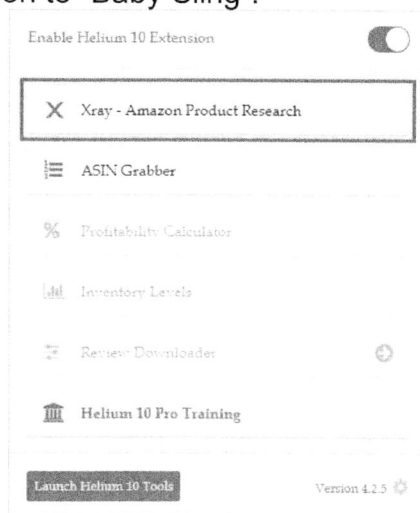

Step #5: As you can observe in the screenshot below, the subcategory "Baby Sling" has a star rating success score of (2) stars, which can be located on the top right-hand side of the launched Xray tool screen:

❖ I have determined that due to the fact that this subcategory has a (2) star rating success score value it is worth my time to continue investigating.

Preparing The Xray Tool For Statistical Data Analysis In A Specific Subcategory:

The next step in statistical data analysis is to prepare Helium 10's Xray tool for product research within the specific keyword phrase you are evaluating. As I stated before, to acquire an approximated idea of whether the specific merchandise you are researching will be profitable for you to retail and whether or not you could succeed entering the specific market you are investigating you should examine the top (1-16) competitors within the specific keyword phrase you are researching. Therefore, for the following (18) lessons devoted to product research I will be illustrating how to perform statistical data analysis by examining the top (1-16) competitors' product listings located within the subcategory "Child Carrier Slings" with the keyword phase "Baby Sling."

As you will learn in the following steps below, each time you perform product research within a specific subcategory or utilizing an exact keyword phrase you must first prepare the Xray tool and organize the statistics provided by Helium 10 into a simplified list that allows you to easily evaluate the top (1-16) competitors' product listing data.

To Prepare The Xray Tool & Organize The Provided Statistics For Data Analysis, follow the instructional steps included with the labeled images below:

Step #1: Navigate to www.amazon.com from within the Google Chrome Web Browser and be sure to have Helium 10's Google Chrome Extension downloaded, installed, and prepared for use as was discussed in Chapter 2.

Step #2: Type the keywords "Baby Sling" into Amazon's search bar and perform a search for the product which will navigate you to a page containing the first (1-48) product listings pertaining to your keyword phrase search entry:

1-48 of 925 results for "baby sling"

Step #3: Once you are navigated to the first page of Amazon product listings containing baby slings you will use your mouse to left-click and release on Helium 10's Google Chrome Extension located on the top right-hand side of the Google Chrome Web Browser which will generate a list of navigational task buttons:

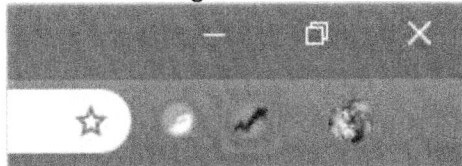

Step #4: Using your mouse, left-click and release on Helium 10's Amazon product research tool Xray which will enable the software to generate your competitions statistical seller data in relation to "Baby Sling":

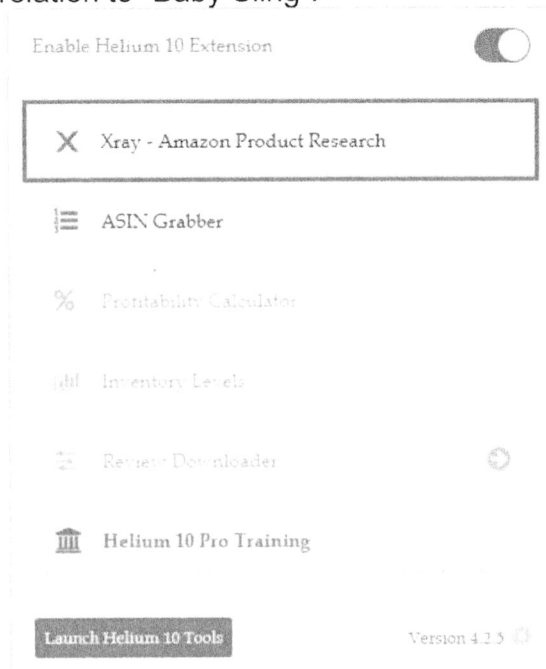

Enable Helium 10 Extension

X   Xray - Amazon Product Research

≣   ASIN Grabber

%   Profitability Calculator

.ıil   Inventory Levels

⟳   Review Downloader

🏛   Helium 10 Pro Training

Launch Helium 10 Tools   Version 4.2.5

Step #5: Using your mouse, use the bar on the right-hand side of the Xray window to scroll down to the very bottom of the list until you reach that very last product listing data provided by Helium 10.

Step #6: Delete each product listing contained in the Xray list up to (#16) until you have a list containing only the top (1-16) competitors' product listing data:

# ▲	ASIN	Brand	Title	Category
1	B005SP2LWW	Boba	SP Boba Wrap Baby Carrier, Grey - ...	Baby
2	B000UZXGCY	Baby K'tan	SP Baby K'tan Original Baby Wrap ...	Baby
3	B00OJVNSFA	Cuddlebug	SP 9-in-1 CuddleBug Baby Wrap Sli...	Baby
4	B005SP2LWW	Boba	Boba Wrap Baby Carrier, Grey - ...	Baby
5	B01AP8R6G2	Kangaroo...	Kangaroobaby Baby Sling Wrap ...	Baby
6	B071FDM61H	Nalakai	Luxury Ring Sling Baby Carrier - ...	Baby
7	B07QPYZMH4	Acrabros	Acrabros Baby Wrap Carrier,Ha...	Baby
8	B00OJVNSFA	Cuddlebug	9-in-1 CuddleBug Baby Wrap Sli...	Baby
9	B012ITTORO	BabyWo...	Baby Wrap Carrier Ring Sling: Ex...	Baby
10	B01CYTYSRO	Sleepy W...	Baby Wrap Ergo Carrier Sling by...	Baby
11	B07MVVTPHP	Cuby	Baby Carrier by Cuby, Natural C...	Baby
12	B07NCNG75J	MEBIEN. ...	Baby Wrap Carrier Ring Sling-Lu...	Baby
13	B07SM127CR	5 STARS ...	Baby Wrap Carrier Sling Holder ...	Baby
14	B01B0SZOYM	Hip Baby ...	Hip Baby Wrap Ring Sling Baby ...	Baby
15	B07DKRXBB5	sweetbee	Lightweight My Honey Wrap - N...	Baby
16	B075SFW83N	Kids N' Su...	4 in 1 Baby Wrap Carrier and Ri...	Baby

Note: To delete a product listing from the provided Xray list simply hover your mouse over the number located on the far left-hand side of the Xray window until a clickable trashcan icon appears. Then using your mouse, left-click and release on the trashcan icon to delete the product listing info from the list:

| 17 | B07SK6GVCJ | Cuby | Cuby Breathable Baby Carrier M... | Baby |

Step #7: Delete each product listing contained in the Xray list that has a blue (SP) Sponsored Ad icon within its title. In this scenario it is the top (1-3) product listings but that will vary on a case by case basis:

# ▲	ASIN	Brand	Title	Category
1	B005SP2LWW	Boba	SP Boba Wrap Baby Carrier, Grey - ...	Baby
2	B000UZXGCY	Baby K'tan	SP Baby K'tan Original Baby Wrap ...	Baby
3	B00OJVNSFA	Cuddlebug	SP 9-in-1 CuddleBug Baby Wrap Sli...	Baby
4	B005SP2LWW	Boba	Boba Wrap Baby Carrier, Grey - ...	Baby
5	B01AP8R6G2	Kangaroo...	Kangaroobaby Baby Sling Wrap ...	Baby
6	B071FDM61H	Nalakai	Luxury Ring Sling Baby Carrier – ...	Baby
7	B07QPYZMH4	Acrabros	Acrabros Baby Wrap Carrier,Ha...	Baby
8	B00OJVNSFA	Cuddlebug	9-in-1 CuddleBug Baby Wrap Sli...	Baby
9	B012ITT0RO	BabyWo...	Baby Wrap Carrier Ring Sling: Ex...	Baby
10	B01CYTYSR0	Sleepy W...	Baby Wrap Ergo Carrier Sling by...	Baby
11	B07MVVTPHP	Cuby	Baby Carrier by Cuby, Natural C...	Baby
12	B07NCNG75J	MEBIEN. ...	Baby Wrap Carrier Ring Sling-Lu...	Baby
13	B07SM127CR	5 STARS ...	Baby Wrap Carrier Sling Holder ...	Baby
14	B01B0SZOYM	Hip Baby ...	Hip Baby Wrap Ring Sling Baby ...	Baby
15	B07DKRXBB5	sweetbee	Lightweight My Honey Wrap - N...	Baby
16	B075SFW83N	Kids N' Su...	4 in 1 Baby Wrap Carrier and Ri...	Baby

*Note: You are deleting the product listings from the Xray list that have a blue (SP) Sponsored Ad icon within their title due to the fact that when conducting statistical data analysis you can acquire a better approximated idea of whether the specific merchandise you are researching will be profitable for you to retail and whether or not you could succeed entering the specific market you are investigating if you solely opt to focus on organically ranking product listings in contrast to inorganically ranking product listings, such is the case with a Sponsored Ad.

*As you can observe in the screenshot below, with exclusion of the (SP) product listings your finalized Xray list that you will utilize for statistical data analysis should contain the top (4-16) product listings:

# ▲	ASIN	Brand	Title	Category
4	B005SP2LWW	Boba	Boba Wrap Baby Carrier, Grey - ...	Baby
5	B01AP8R6G2	Kangaroo...	Kangaroobaby Baby Sling Wrap ...	Baby
6	B071FDM61H	Nalakai	Luxury Ring Sling Baby Carrier - ...	Baby
7	B07QPYZMH4	Acrabros	Acrabros Baby Wrap Carrier,Ha...	Baby
8	B00OJVNSFA	Cuddlebug	9-in-1 CuddleBug Baby Wrap Sli...	Baby
9	B012ITT0RO	BabyWo...	Baby Wrap Carrier Ring Sling: Ex...	Baby
10	B01CYTYSR0	Sleepy W...	Baby Wrap Ergo Carrier Sling by...	Baby
11	B07MVVTPHP	Cuby	Baby Carrier by Cuby, Natural C...	Baby
12	B07NCNG75J	MEBIEN. ...	Baby Wrap Carrier Ring Sling-Lu...	Baby
13	B07SM127CR	5 STARS ...	Baby Wrap Carrier Sling Holder ...	Baby
14	B01B0SZOYM	Hip Baby ...	Hip Baby Wrap Ring Sling Baby ...	Baby
15	B07DKRXBB5	sweetbee	Lightweight My Honey Wrap - N...	Baby
16	B075SFW83N	Kids N' Su...	4 in 1 Baby Wrap Carrier and Ri...	Baby

Step #8: Using your mouse, in the same manner that you would with a web browser, expand the Xray window to the right side of the screen until it is fully open so that you can view all of the provided statistics for the top (1-16) competitors' product listings or in this case the top (4-16) with exclusion of the (SP) product listings that you deleted.

❖ Within The Expanded Xray Window You Should Now Be Able To Observe The Following List Of Information For The Top (1-16) Competitors' Product Listings Or In This Case The Top (4-16) With Exclusion Of The (SP) Product Listings That You Deleted:

In Order From Left To Right:

- Product Listing Rank Position
- (ASIN)
- Brand Name
- Product Listing Title
- Primary Category
- BuyBox Owner
- # Of Sellers
- Fulfillment Method
- Product Listing Price Point
- (FBA) Fee
- Sales Volume
- Sales Charts
- Total Revenue
- (BSR)
- Customer Star Rating Value
- Review Count
- Review Velocity
- Product Dimensions
- Product Weight
- Size Tier
- Number Of Product Listing Images

❖ You have now completed the task of preparing the Xray tool and organizing the provided statistics for data analysis.

Criteria Checklist To Utilize When Conducting Statistical Data Analysis:

The next step in statistical data analysis is to scrutinize the information you prepared and organized in the previous lesson by working through each aspect of the following criteria checklist. If a product meets at least (75%) of the recommended requirements from the criteria checklist, which is a result of (13/17) passing, then the merchandise you are researching has the potential to be a viable profitable option for you to source from a supplier, have manufactured, and retail on Amazon.

Please be aware, that although I can provide you with the following criteria checklist, illustrate the methods of working through it within the following exercises, and ultimately teach you how to properly conduct product discovery, your successfulness as an Amazon Seller will rely heavily on other factors as well. What I mean by this statement is that, although locating a viable profitable product to retail is a large piece of solving the Amazon puzzle, it is only one piece. There are many more tasks to work through post product discovery to effectively construct a complete puzzle and successfully retail merchandise on the Amazon Marketplace.

Note: The criteria checklist provided below is not specific to one type of keyword phrase, such as the "Baby Sling" example being utilized in these lessons. The checklist can be used repeatedly on any product, keyword phrase, or subcategory of your choice when you need to determine its level of third-party seller competition, (BSR), popularity among customers, projected per unit sales, and profitability margins.

1) At Least (10) Out Of The Top (16) Competitors Have A Customer Review Count Of Less Than (500). *Order by Review Count.*

2) At Least (6) Out Of The Top (16) Competitors Have A Customer Star Rating Value Of Less Than (4). *-Organise by Ratings high to low*

3) At Least (4) Out Of The Top (16) Competitors Have A (BSR) Of (10,000) Or Less.

4) The Top Competitor Out Of (1-16) Has At Least (3) Organically Ranking Keyword Phrases With A Monthly Search Volume Of No Less Than (5,000) Each That Places Their Product Listing On Page (1) Of Generated Search Results.
order either by No. or Sales - Take top ASIN - H10 - Cerebro + paste first keywords - notes

5) The Top Competitor Has At Least (10) Organically Ranking Keyword Phrases With A Monthly Search Volume Of No Less Than (600) Each That Places Their Product Listing On Page (1) Of Generated Search Results.

6) At Least (8) Out Of The Top (16) Competitors Have A Helium 10 Product Listing Evaluation Result Of (9) Or Less. *shows on LHS of main image on Product Listing shows as Evaluation result 10 of 10*

7) At Least (8) Out Of The Top (16) Competitors Product Listings Are Less Than (2) Years Old. *Go into Sales - All Time - Look at graph*

8) At Least (8) Out Of The Top (16) Competitors Have Experienced Either Increasing Or Stable Sales Volume For No Less Than A Year. *as' -change to 1 YEAR*
if seasonal look at season to check consistent sales

9) Total Monthly Sales Volume For The Top (16) Competitors Must Be Greater Than (3,000) Units. *Add up Sales column, total should be greater than 3000*
elooking for

10) At Least (6) Out Of The Top (16) Competitors Generate A Total Monthly Sales *10 sales a day* Volume Of No Less Than (300) Units. *Sort by Sales column = units*

11) At Least (6) Out Of The Top (16) Competitors Generate A Yearly Total Sales Volume Of No Less Than (3600) Units.
Go into Sales graph - #YEAR - look at sales + roughly add of sold units
Hard for seasonal products

One out of top 16 competitors

12) (1) Out Of The Top (16) Competitors Does Not Make Up More Than (75%) Of The Total Monthly Sales Volume. *Add up sales column x .75. check no comp is close to that figure*

13) Less Than Half Of The Top (16) Competitors Are Recognizable Brand Names Or Well-Established Mainstream Companies. *Google - what are top US brand names for light energy lamps, look for big brand like Phillips*

14) Ability To Differentiate The Product By Adding A Feature To It That Makes The Merchandise More Functional For The Consumer Or Provides A Sense Of Perceived Value In Contrast To The Top (16) Competitors. *Go into product listing + look for added bits that differenciate. check faqs. review first.*

15) The Top (16) Competitors Have Noticeable Differences In Their Product Listing Price Points. *Look at Price Column*

16) Ability To Retail The Product For No Less Than (5x) The Landing Costs. *Shipping / FNSKU Labels / Inspection / Labour*

17) Ability To Generate A Gross Profitability Margin Of No Less Than (30%). *— See P. 112*

(17) Methods Of Conducting Statistical Data Analysis Utilizing The Criteria Checklist:

Note: Please be aware, that the Amazon product listing data supplied by Helium 10 updates on a daily and monthly basis therefore when you work through the following (17) exercises do not be dissuaded if the statistics offered to you appear different from what is printed in the lessons.

 ❖ For the following (17) methods of conducting statistical data analysis I will be utilizing the Xray information containing the top (1-16) competitors with exclusion of the (3) (SP) product listings for the keyword phrase "Baby Sling" that were prepared, organized, and finalized in a previous lesson.

Method #1: Determining That At Least (10) Out Of The Top (16) Competitors Have A Customer Review Count Of Less Than (500).

One subject you must comprehend when researching merchandise to retail is the ideology that customers buying products on Amazon typically tend to rely heavily on reading previous customer's product listing reviews to help guide them in their purchasing decision, which means that when a consumer is searching for a specific product to purchase they are much more inclined to buy their items from a seller's listing that has a high-review count in contrast to procuring their goods from a seller with a low-review count. What this means to you as an Amazon Seller is that if (10) of your top (16) competitors have a customer review count of more than (500) they are already dominating the market within the specific subcategory or keyword phrase you are researching which will make it difficult for you to procure sales selling a similar product due to the fact that your product will have (0) reviews when it is first listed. I am not saying that it is impossible to enter the specific market and retail similar products as those of your competitors that have a high-review count, but it will be tough to compete with these long-term seasoned sellers. Ultimately, it takes product sales to acquire customer reviews and vice versa. If you do not have a chance to procure sales from your product listing due to your competition already dominating the particular product market you are attempting to enter then there is no chance to obtain customer reviews. Therefore, as you locate potential products to retail the first step of statistical data analysis should be focused on determining the level of third-party competition that you would face on Amazon. I recommend locating the first (1-16) of your top competitor's listings on Amazon within the subcategory or keyword phrase you are researching and verifying their review count. If you determine that your top (10) competitors have a review count of (500) or more I suggest locating and opting to retail a product that has a lower level of competition.

*As you can observe in the screenshot below, through utilization of Helium 10's Amazon product research tool Xray you can quickly and easily individually investigate the top (1-16) competitors' total review counts. Furthermore, upon examination of the provided data I have concluded that (10) out of the top (1-16) competitors utilizing the keyword phrase "Baby Sling" have less than (500) reviews, therefore it passes criteria checklist point (#1):

Review Count
17
104
135
215
272
384
401
429
468
498
1,000
3,057
4,712

*Note: If you are working along on your computer you may have noticed that your review amounts were not initially in order from least to greatest as they appear in the image above. Please be aware, that you can organize any column of data within Xray from least to greatest and vice versa by simply clicking the column title as can be observed in the screenshot below:

Review Count
17
104
135
215
272
384
401
429
468
498
1,000
3,057
4,712

Method #2: Determining That At Least (6) Out Of The Top (16) Competitors Have A Customer Star Rating Value Of Less Than (4).

Similarly to the manner that reviews operate, customers buying products on Amazon typically tend to rely heavily on viewing previous customer's star rating levels to help guide them in their purchasing decision, which means that when a consumer is searching for a specific product to purchase they are much more inclined to buy their merchandise from a seller's listing that has a large amount of high-star ratings in contrast to procuring their goods from a seller with a small amount of low-star ratings. What this means to you as an Amazon Seller is that if (6) of your top (16) competitors have a customer star-rating level of 4 stars and above they are already dominating the market within the specific subcategory or keyword phrase you are researching which will make it difficult for you to procure sales selling a similar product due to the fact that your product will have (0) star ratings when it is first listed. I am not stating that it is impossible to enter the specific market and retail similar products as those of your competitors that have a high-star level, but it will be tough to compete with these long-term seasoned sellers. Ultimately, it takes product sales to acquire customer star ratings and vice versa. If you do not have a chance to procure sales from your product listing due to your competition already dominating the particular product market you are attempting to enter then there is no chance to obtain customer star ratings. Therefore, as you locate potential products to retail the second step of statistical data analysis should be focused on further determining the level of third-party competition that you would face on Amazon. I recommend locating the first (1-16) of your top competitor's listings on Amazon within the subcategory or keyword phrase you are researching and verifying their star rating level. If you determine that your top (6) competitors have a star rating level of (4) or more I suggest locating and opting to retail a product that has a lower level of competition.

*As you can observe in the screenshot below, through utilization of Helium 10's Amazon product research tool Xray you can quickly and easily individually investigate the top (1-16) competitors' customer star rating values. Furthermore, upon examination of the provided data I have concluded that (6) out of the top (1-16) competitors utilizing the keyword phrase "Baby Sling" have less than a (4) star customer rating value, therefore it passes criteria checklist point (#2):

Rating ▲
3.5
3.5
3.5
3.5
3.5
3.5
4.5
4.5
4.5
4.5
4.5
4.5
5

Pro Tip:

Another aspect to focus on as you research your level of third-party seller competition is whether or not your top competitor's customer reviews and star ratings are mostly positive or primarily negative. Clearly it will be much easier to compete with top competitors that have more than (500) customer reviews if they are negative and the seller has a low (1-3) star rating in contrast to top competitor's with over (500) positive customer reviews and a high (4-5) star rating due to the fact that you could make the necessary changes to the product that is causing your competitors to receive negative reviews and low star ratings. Therefore, as you investigate your top competitor's review counts do not exclusively focus on the amount of customer reviews each has and their star rating levels but also be sure to read through their reviews to determine whether they are mostly positive or primarily negative. You may be able to compete with top level third-party sellers that have a large volume of negative reviews by supplying customers with an alternative choice to purchase a better developed higher quality product with added features sold at a lower price point than that of your competitors. By utilizing the tactic of retailing a higher quality product at a lower price point you would then be able to procure enough sales to obtain the amount of reviews it takes to compete leading to you potentially being able to dominate the product market you are entering. You could then opt to gradually increase your product price point since your merchandise offers added value.

Method #3: Determining That At Least (4) Out Of The Top (16) Competitors Have A (BSR) Of (10,000) Or Less.

An integral aspect of statistical data analysis focuses on investigating the popularity of the merchandise among customers on Amazon. A direct result of procuring consumer sales relies on the demand of the product you intend to market. If a product is in high-demand it means it procures a large volume of sales and vice versa.

A low (BSR) when you are researching a specific keyword phrase or subcategory indicates high-demand for the product you are investigating and vice versa therefore an essential component of statistical data analysis relies on evaluating your top (1-16) competitors' (BSRs).

*As you can observe in the screenshot below, through utilization of Helium 10's Amazon product research tool Xray you can quickly and easily individually investigate the top (1-16) competitors' (BSRs). Furthermore, upon examination of the provided data I have concluded that (9) out of the top (1-16) competitors utilizing the keyword phrase "Baby Sling" have a (BSR) of less than (10,000), therefore it passes criteria checklist point (#3):

BSR 📈 ▲
112
623
1,125
1,289
3,468
5,786
5,798
6,197
8,318
11,281
12,304
16,637
48,021

Method #4: Determining That The Top Competitor Out Of (1-16) Has At Least (3) Organically Ranking Keyword Phrases With A Monthly Search Volume Of No Less Than (5,000) Each That Places Their Product Listing On Page (1) Of Generated Search Results.

In similarity to (BSR), Method #4 can be utilized as an approximated indication that there is high-demand for the product you are researching. Furthermore, and more importantly, it also tells you that the seller is organically driving large amounts of traffic to their product listing on separate Amazon pages of generated search results through the use of a combination of high-ranking keyword phrases in contrast to solely one high-ranking keyword phrase and one Amazon page of generated search results. What this means to you as an Amazon Seller, is that there are several high-ranking keyword phrases that you can utilize to build your product listing & potentially bid on when you run (PPC) Sponsored Ad Campaigns that will drive traffic to your product listing on separate Amazon pages of generated search results.

Ultimately, the primary purpose of evaluating this information in this scenario is to investigate how much opportunity there is for you to compete with the other sellers and how many Amazon pages of generated search results you can try to rank on page one for.

A clearer way to illustrate the importance of evaluating this data is through the use of simple mathematics.

As you can observe in the chart below, the product "Baby Sling" has (5) organically high-ranking keyword phrases that customers utilize to locate this particular product each driving them to (5) separate Amazon product listing pages, which means there is (5) high-traffic opportunities for you to retail your merchandise. Now imagine that there was only one high-ranking keyword phrase for the product "Baby Sling." That would mean that there would only be one Amazon product listing page to retail your product on and all of the competitors from the chart below would be competing for the number one spot thus making it much harder to procure sales in contrast to the distribution observed in the screenshot below:

#		Phrase	Cerebro IQ Score	Search Volume	Sponsored ASINs	Competing Products
1	✗	baby carrier ☑ Amazon's Choice	80,799	80,799	233	>1,000
2	✗	baby wrap carrier ☑ Amazon's Choice	24,038	13,389	253	>557
3	✗	baby sling ☑	11,625	10,718	282	>922
4	✗	baby wrap ☑ Amazon's Choice	15,694	10,609	321	>676
5	✗	baby carrier wrap ☑ Amazon's Choice	13,725	7,631	261	>556

To Determine That The Top Competitor Out Of (1-16) Has At Least (3) Organically Ranking Keyword Phrases With A Monthly Search Volume Of No Less Than (5,000) Each, follow the instructional steps included with the labeled images below:

Step #1: Using your mouse, left-click and release on the top competitor's (ASIN) for "Baby Sling" from the Xray list created in a previous lesson to navigate to the product listing detail page:

# ▲	ASIN	Brand	Title	Category
4	B005SP2LWW	Boba	Boba Wrap Baby Carrier, Grey - ...	Baby
5	B01AP8R6G2	Kangaroo...	Kangaroobaby Baby Sling Wrap ...	Baby
6	B071FDM61H	Nalakai	Luxury Ring Sling Baby Carrier - ...	Baby
7	B07QPYZMH4	Acrabros	Acrabros Baby Wrap Carrier,Ha...	Baby
8	B00OJVNSFA	Cuddlebug	9-in-1 CuddleBug Baby Wrap Sli...	Baby
9	B012ITT0RO	BabyWo...	Baby Wrap Carrier Ring Sling: Ex...	Baby
10	B01CYTYSR0	Sleepy W...	Baby Wrap Ergo Carrier Sling by...	Baby
11	B07MVVTPHP	Cuby	Baby Carrier by Cuby, Natural C...	Baby
12	B07NCNG75J	MEBIEN. ...	Baby Wrap Carrier Ring Sling-Lu...	Baby
13	B07SM127CR	5 STARS ...	Baby Wrap Carrier Sling Holder ...	Baby
14	B01B0SZOYM	Hip Baby ...	Hip Baby Wrap Ring Sling Baby ...	Baby
15	B07DKRXBB5	sweetbee	Lightweight My Honey Wrap - N...	Baby
16	B075SFW83N	Kids N' Su...	4 in 1 Baby Wrap Carrier and Ri...	Baby

*Note: Within Step #1 you will always choose the (ASIN) from top (1-16) competitors who has sold the most units, which happened to be in the #1 spot within the Xray list I created for this lesson, but that will not always be the case therefore be sure to check each (ASINs) monthly unit sales total:

# ▲	ASIN	Brand	Title	Category	BuyBox	# �∎		Price	FBA fee	Sales
4	B005SP2LWW	Boba	Boba Wrap Baby Carrier, Grey - ...	Baby	Boba Inc. (USA)	1	FBA	$39.95	$11.25	9,688

Step #2: Using your mouse scroll down the product listing detail page until you locate the Helium 10 tool bar. Then using your mouse, left-click and release on the "Keywords" icon to be navigated to the "Reverse ASIN Lookup" tool Cerebro within the Helium 10 dashboard:

🎯	🗐 Inventory Levels	✕ Xray	🌐 Keywords	🗔 Listing Optimizer	% Profitability Calculator

OR:

Copy/Paste the top competitor's (ASIN) from their product listing directly into the Cerebro tool located on the Helium 10 dashboard.

Step #3: In the filters section within the Cerebro dashboard enter a search volume minimum of 5000:

Search Volume ⑦

5000   -   Max

Step #4: In the filters section within the Cerebro dashboard enter an organic rank minimum of 1 and a maximum of 16:

Organic Rank ⑦

1   -   16

Step #5: In the filters section within the Cerebro dashboard enter a word count minimum of 2:

Word count ⑦

2   -   Max

Step #6: Using your mouse, left-click and release on the apply button located on the right-hand side of the Cerebro dashboard:

✖ Clear Filters   Apply

Step #7: In the default tab within the Cerebro dashboard choose the option "Search Volume High To Low":

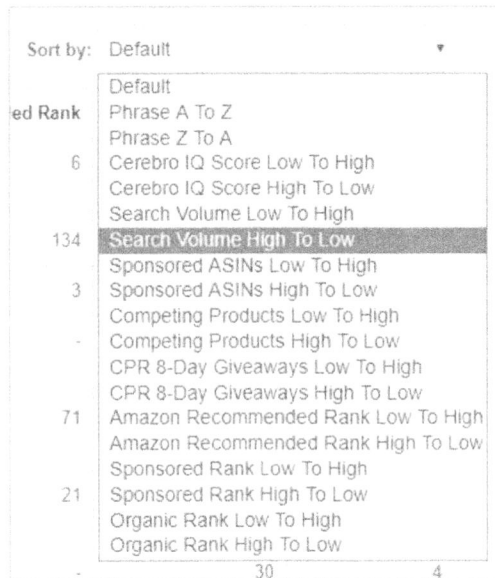

Step #8: In the filtered keywords section within the Cerebro dashboard use the clickable X icon located on the left-hand side of keyword phrase to delete any brand names or unrelatable keyword phrases from the generated list:

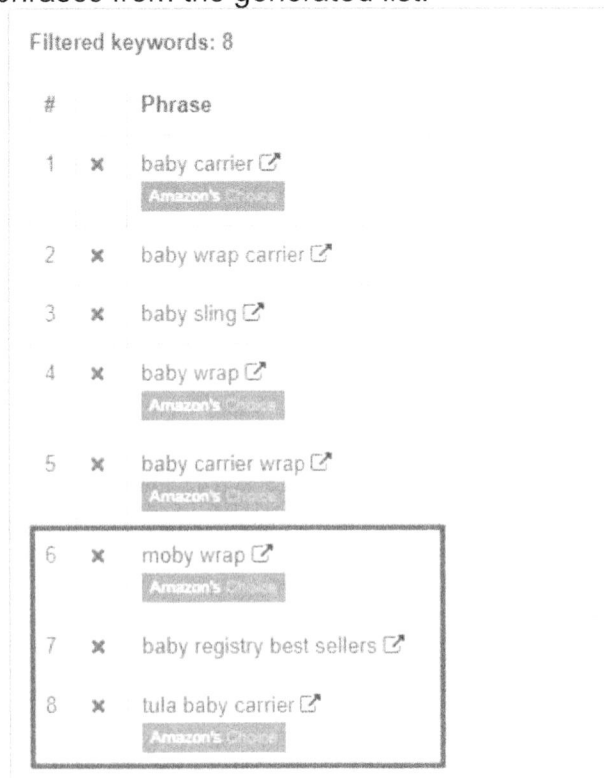

*As you can observe in the screenshot below, upon examination of the provided data I have obtained from Helium 10's Cerebro tool I have concluded that the top competitor out of (1-16) has at least (3) organically ranking keyword phrases with a monthly search volume of no less than (5,000) each, therefore it passes criteria checklist point (#4):

Phrase	Cerebro IQ Score	Search Volume
baby carrier ☑ Amazon's Choice	80,799	80,799
baby wrap carrier ☑	37,295	13,389
baby sling ☑	11,625	10,718
baby wrap ☑ Amazon's Choice	3,536	10,609
baby carrier wrap ☑ Amazon's Choice	12,956	7,631

Method #5: Determining That The Top Competitor Has At Least (10) Organically Ranking Keyword Phrases With A Monthly Search Volume Of No Less Than (600) Each That Places Their Product Listing On Page (1) Of Generated Search Results.

Method #5 can be utilized to tell you that the seller is organically driving traffic to their product listing on separate Amazon pages of generated search results through the use of a combination of low-ranking keyword phrases in contrast to solely the high-ranking keyword phrases from Method #4. What this means to you as an Amazon Seller is that there are several low-ranking keyword phrases that you can utilize to build your product listing & potentially bid on when you run (PPC) Sponsored Ad Campaigns that will drive traffic to your product listing on separate Amazon pages of generated search results.

Ultimately, the primary purpose of evaluating this information in this scenario is to investigate how much extra opportunity there is for you to compete with the other sellers and how many Amazon pages of generated search results you can try to rank on page one for without having to focus solely on the competitive high-ranking keywords from Method #4. Furthermore, running (PPC) Sponsored Ad Campaigns can be costly, but if you bid on some of these lower ranking keywords it will be much less expensive, especially during your product launch phase. You could then plan for the future with intentions of working your way towards ranking to page one of generated search results for some of the high-ranking keywords from Method #4.

To Determine That The Top Competitor Out (1-16) Has At Least (10) Organically Ranking Keyword Phrases With A Monthly Search Volume Of No Less Than (600) Each, follow the instructional steps included with the labeled images below:

Step #1: Using your mouse, left-click and release on the top competitor's (ASIN) for "Baby Sling" from the Xray list created in a previous lesson to navigate to the product listing detail page:

# ▲	ASIN	Brand	Title	Category
4	B005SP2LWW	Boba	Boba Wrap Baby Carrier, Grey - ...	Baby
5	B01AP8R6G2	Kangaroo...	Kangaroobaby Baby Sling Wrap ...	Baby
6	B071FDM61H	Nalakai	Luxury Ring Sling Baby Carrier - ...	Baby
7	B07QPYZMH4	Acrabros	Acrabros Baby Wrap Carrier,Ha...	Baby
8	B00OJVNSFA	Cuddlebug	9-in-1 CuddleBug Baby Wrap Sli...	Baby
9	B012ITTORO	BabyWo...	Baby Wrap Carrier Ring Sling: Ex...	Baby
10	B01CYTYSR0	Sleepy W...	Baby Wrap Ergo Carrier Sling by...	Baby
11	B07MVVTPHP	Cuby	Baby Carrier by Cuby, Natural C...	Baby
12	B07NCNG75J	MEBIEN. ...	Baby Wrap Carrier Ring Sling-Lu...	Baby
13	B07SM127CR	5 STARS ...	Baby Wrap Carrier Sling Holder ...	Baby
14	B01B0SZOYM	Hip Baby ...	Hip Baby Wrap Ring Sling Baby ...	Baby
15	B07DKRXBB5	sweetbee	Lightweight My Honey Wrap - N...	Baby
16	B075SFW83N	Kids N' Su...	4 in 1 Baby Wrap Carrier and Ri...	Baby

Step #2: Using your mouse scroll down the product listing detail page until you locate the Helium 10 tool bar. Then using your mouse, left-click and release on the "Keywords" icon to be navigated to the "Reverse ASIN Lookup" tool Cerebro within the Helium 10 dashboard:

✅	🗂 Inventory Levels	✕ Xray	⚙ Keywords	🗐 Listing Optimizer	% Profitability Calculator

OR:

Copy/Paste the top competitor's (ASIN) from their product listing directly into the Cerebro tool located on the Helium 10 dashboard.

Step #3: In the filters section within the Cerebro dashboard enter a search volume minimum of 600 and a maximum of 4999:

Search Volume ⑦

600   4999

Step #4: In the filters section within the Cerebro dashboard enter an organic rank minimum of 1 and a maximum of 16:

Organic Rank ⑦

1   -   16

Step #5: In the filters section within the Cerebro dashboard enter a word count minimum of 2:

Word count ⑦

2   -   Max

Step #6: Using your mouse, left-click and release on the apply button located on the right-hand side of the Cerebro dashboard:

✖ Clear Filters | Apply

Step #7: In the default tab within the Cerebro dashboard choose the option "Search Volume High To Low":

Sort by: Default   ▼

	Default
ed Rank	Phrase A To Z
	Phrase Z To A
6	Cerebro IQ Score Low To High
	Cerebro IQ Score High To Low
	Search Volume Low To High
134	Search Volume High To Low
	Sponsored ASINs Low To High
3	Sponsored ASINs High To Low
	Competing Products Low To High
-	Competing Products High To Low
	CPR 8-Day Giveaways Low To High
	CPR 8-Day Giveaways High To Low
71	Amazon Recommended Rank Low To High
	Amazon Recommended Rank High To Low
	Sponsored Rank Low To High
21	Sponsored Rank High To Low
	Organic Rank Low To High
	Organic Rank High To Low
-	30 4

Step #8: In the filtered keywords section within the Cerebro dashboard begin at the top of the list and use the clickable X icon located on the left-hand side of keyword phrase to delete any brand names or unrelatable keyword phrases from the generated list until you have at least (10) organically ranking keyword phrases with a monthly search volume of no less than (600).

*As you can observe in the screenshot below, upon examination of the provided data I have obtained from Helium 10's Cerebro tool I have concluded that the top competitor out of (1-16) has at least (10) organically ranking keyword phrases with a monthly search volume of no less than (600) each, therefore it passes criteria checklist point (#5):

Phrase	Cerebro IQ Score	Search Volume
infant carrier	4,211	3,925
baby carriers	3,225	3,225
baby sling carrier	4,785	2,919
baby slings and wraps	5,781	2,642
newborn carrier	4,466	2,327
baby holder carrier	5,767	1,955
baby holder	195	1,948
baby wraps	46	1,851
baby carrier sling	2,784	1,687
baby wraps and slings	4,954	1,516

Method #6: Determining That At Least (8) Out Of The Top (16) Competitors Have A Helium 10 Product Listing Evaluation Result Of (9) Or Less.

For this task you will be individually navigating to each of the top (1-16) competitors and determining their Helium 10 product listing evaluation result. The reason for performing this procedure is to review their product listings to observe whether or not the majority of them are sophisticated, well-optimized, and successfully built. If at least (8) out of the top (16) competitors have poorly constructed product listings with an evaluation result of (9) or less then you may be able to gain a competitive edge by building a much more sophisticated product listing that will make consumers opt to purchase your product over that of your rivals. If the opposite was the case and (8) out of the top (16) competitors have elegant product listings you lose the extra advantage because consumers have numerous well-optimized product listings to choose from, which means yours is among many. With that said, you should always attempt to have an extremely tasteful product listing even if your competitors fail to do so. The topic of building sophisticated product listings will be comprehensively covered in subsequent chapters.

Checklist To Utilize When Evaluating Product Listings:

- The quality of their images.
- Are their image dimensions the Amazon recommend (1000x1000) pixels.
- Did they utilize each image slot?
- Does their main image aka lead image have a white background?
- Does their title contain the full (150) characters allowed & is it well-written?
- Do they have 5 bullet points & are they well-written?
- Does their description contain the full (2000) characters allowed & is it well-written?
- Does their product listing have (EBC) Enhanced Brand Content which means they are Brand Registered?
- Is their customer star rating level score a (4) or higher?
- Is their customer review count higher than (10)?

To Navigate To Each Of The Top (1-16) Competitors Product Listings To Determine Their Product Listing Evaluation Result, follow the instructional steps included with the labeled images below:

Step #1: Using your mouse, left-click and release on the top competitor's (ASIN) for "Baby Sling" from the Xray list created in a previous lesson to navigate to the product listing detail page:

# ▲	ASIN	Brand	Title	Category
4	B005SP2LWW	Boba	Boba Wrap Baby Carrier, Grey - ...	Baby
5	B01AP8R6G2	Kangaroo...	Kangaroobaby Baby Sling Wrap ...	Baby
6	B071FDM61H	Nalakai	Luxury Ring Sling Baby Carrier – ...	Baby
7	B07QPYZMH4	Acrabros	Acrabros Baby Wrap Carrier,Ha...	Baby
8	B00OJVNSFA	Cuddlebug	9-in-1 CuddleBug Baby Wrap Sli...	Baby
9	B012ITT0RO	BabyWo...	Baby Wrap Carrier Ring Sling: Ex...	Baby
10	B01CYTYSR0	Sleepy W...	Baby Wrap Ergo Carrier Sling by...	Baby
11	B07MVVTPHP	Cuby	Baby Carrier by Cuby, Natural C...	Baby
12	B07NCNG75J	MEBIEN. ...	Baby Wrap Carrier Ring Sling-Lu...	Baby
13	B07SM127CR	5 STARS ...	Baby Wrap Carrier Sling Holder ...	Baby
14	B01B0SZOYM	Hip Baby ...	Hip Baby Wrap Ring Sling Baby ...	Baby
15	B07DKRXBB5	sweetbee	Lightweight My Honey Wrap - N...	Baby
16	B075SFW83N	Kids N' Su...	4 in 1 Baby Wrap Carrier and Ri...	Baby

Step #2: As you can observe in the screenshot below, the evaluation result will appear in the top left-hand side of the product details page directly above the lead image:

❖ Repeat this same task for the remainder of the top (1-16) competitors' product listings from the Xray list.

*Upon examination of each of the top (1-16) competitors' product listing evaluation results I have concluded that only (5) have a score of less than (9), therefore it fails criteria checklist point (#6).

Method #7: Determining That At Least (8) Out Of The Top (16) Competitors Product Listings Are Less Than (2) Years Old.

For this task you will be individually navigating to each of the top (1-16) competitors and determining the age of their product listings. The reason for performing this procedure is to verify the overall age of the market. If (8) out of the top (16) competitors product listings are over (2) years old then it is a sign that this market is mature, which means most of top sellers are well-established. This will make it more difficult to compete and gain traction as a new seller first entering the market due to the fact that the other sellers are most likely already dominating.

To Determine If Your Top (1-16) Competitors' Product Listings Are Less Than (2) Years Old, follow the instructional steps included with the labeled images below:

Step #1: Using your mouse, left-click and release on the top competitor's sales graph for "Baby Sling" from the Xray list created in a previous lesson to navigate to their sales chart:

Step #2: Using your mouse, left-click and release on the "All Time" navigational task button:

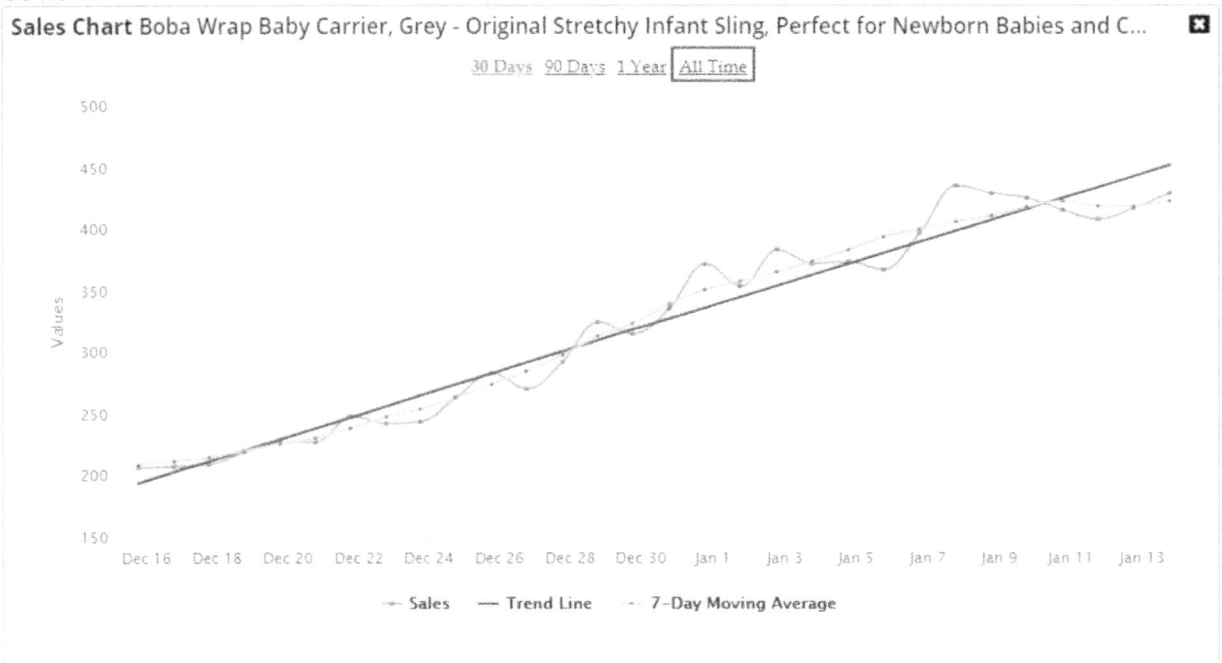

Step #3: Using your mouse, scroll without clicking, over to far left-hand side of the sales chart until the data appears. As you can observe in the screenshot below, this seller's product listing has been live on Amazon since 1/14/2018, which means they have been retailing this specific product since that date:

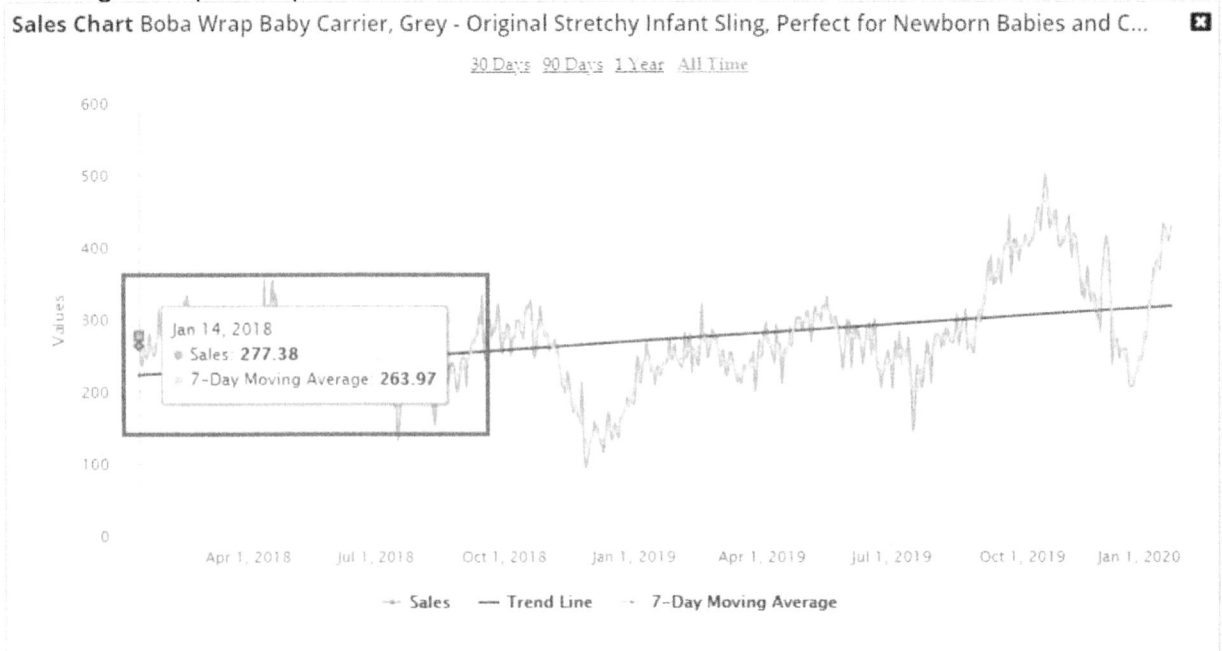

❖ Repeat this same task for the remainder of the top (1-16) competitors' product listings from the Xray list.

*Upon examination of each of the top (1-16) competitors' product listings age I have concluded that (13) are under (2) years old, therefore it passes criteria checklist point (#7).

Method #8: Determining That At Least (8) Out Of The Top (16) Competitors Have Experienced Either Increasing Or Stable Sales Volume For No Less Than A Year.

For this task you will be individually navigating to each of the top (1-16) competitors and determining whether or not their sales have been increasing or at least remained stable for the last year. The reason for performing this procedure is to verify that this market is not a trend that is on the decline and that the product remains in demand throughout the year. If (8) out of the top (16) competitors product listings were decreasing in sales or generally unstable it may be due to a failing market or a seasonal product. I would never recommend retailing a product whose sales history is on the decline due to the fact that you would have a difficult time competing for buyers with the seasoned sellers as the market fails. Furthermore, there is no market longevity with a failing product or future promise of success.

To Determine If Your Top (1-16) Competitors' Product Listings Have Experienced Either Increasing Or Stable Sales Volume For No Less Than A Year, follow the instructional steps included with the labeled images below:

Step #1: Using your mouse, left-click and release on the top competitor's sales graph for "Baby Sling" from the Xray list created in a previous lesson to navigate to their sales chart:

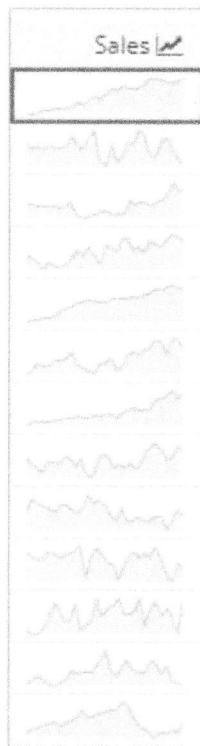

Step #2: Using your mouse, left-click and release on the "1 Year" navigational task button:

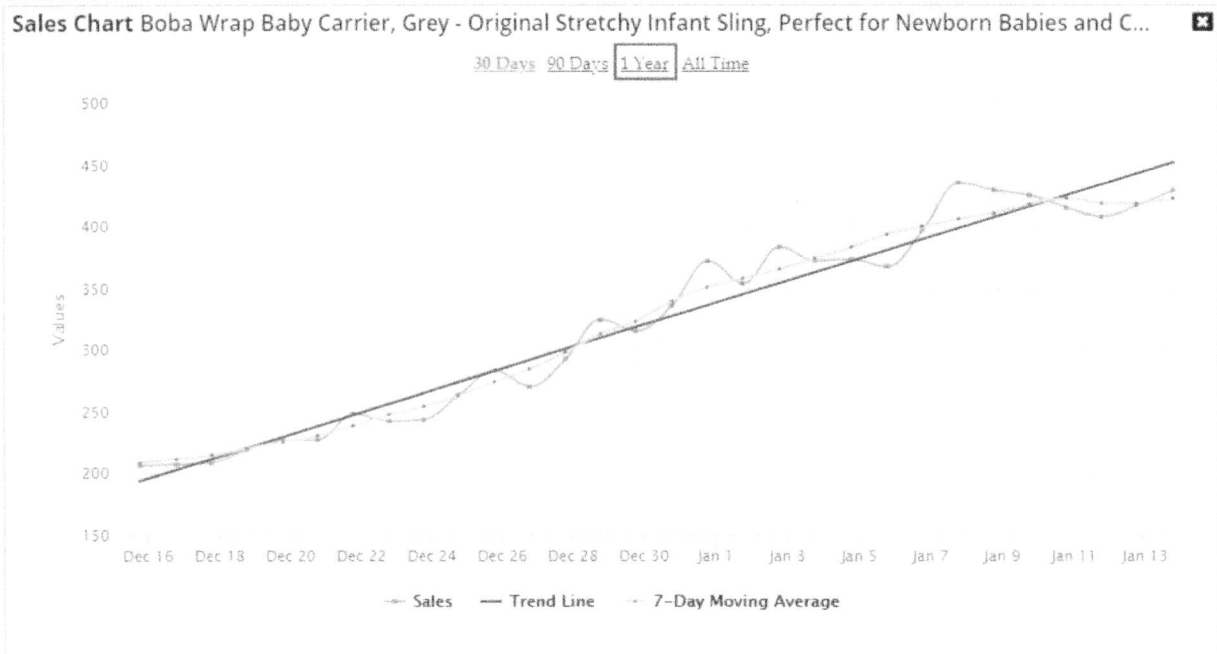

Sales Chart Boba Wrap Baby Carrier, Grey - Original Stretchy Infant Sling, Perfect for Newborn Babies and C... ❎

30 Days 90 Days 1 Year All Time

Sales — Trend Line — 7-Day Moving Average

Step #3: Examine the sales chart to determine whether or not the sales volume is decreasing, steady, or increasing:

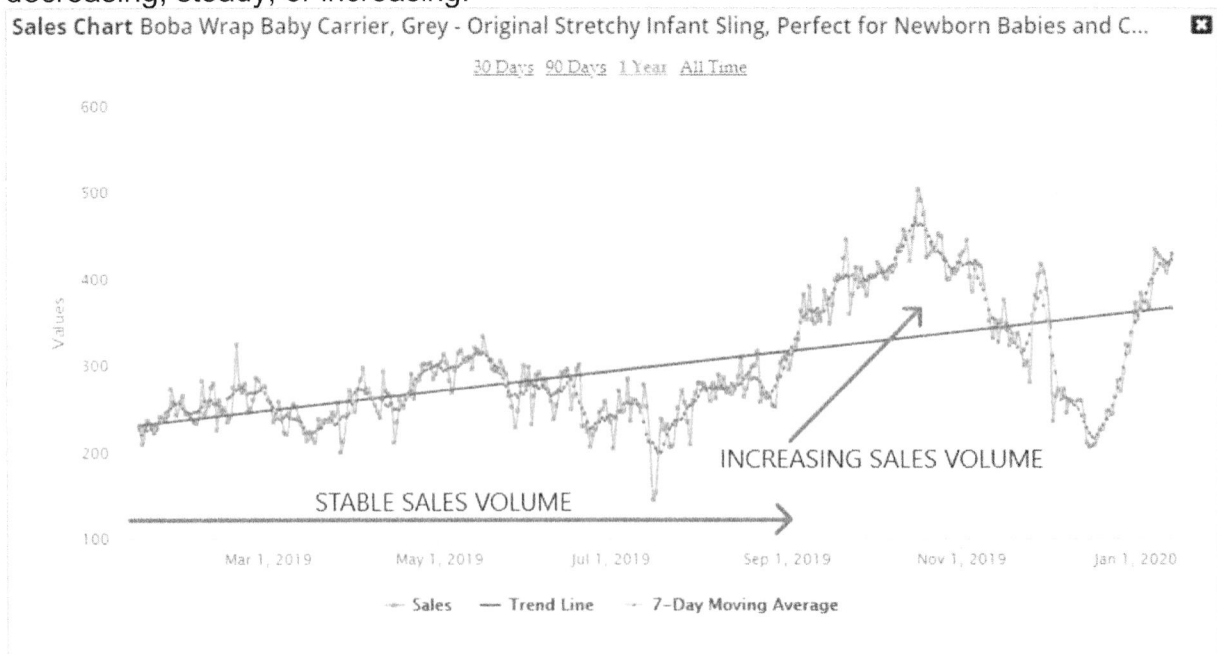

Sales Chart Boba Wrap Baby Carrier, Grey - Original Stretchy Infant Sling, Perfect for Newborn Babies and C... ❎

30 Days 90 Days 1 Year All Time

STABLE SALES VOLUME

INCREASING SALES VOLUME

Sales — Trend Line — 7-Day Moving Average

❖ Repeat this same task for the remainder of the top (1-16) competitors' product listings from the Xray list.

*Upon examination of each of the top (1-16) competitors' product listings yearly sales volume statistics I have concluded that (13) are steady or increasing, therefore it passes criteria checklist point (#8).

Method #9: Determining That The Total Monthly Sales Volume For The Top (16) Competitors Is Greater Than (3,000) Units.

For this task you will be adding up the total monthly sales volume of the top (1-16) competitors and determining whether that value is greater or less than (3,000) units. The reason for performing this procedure is to verify if the product is in demand. I will reiterate the fact that an integral aspect of statistical data analysis focuses on investigating the popularity of the merchandise among customers on Amazon. A direct result of procuring consumer sales relies on the demand of the product you intend to market. If a product is in high-demand it means it procures a large volume of sales and vice versa. If you conclude that the total monthly sales volume for the top (16) competitors is greater than (3,000) it indicates high-demand for the product you are researching.

*As you can observe in the screenshot below, through utilization of Helium 10's Amazon product research tool Xray you can quickly and easily individually investigate the top (1-16) competitors' total monthly unit sales volume. Furthermore, upon examination of the provided data I have concluded that the total sales volume of the top (1-16) competitors is greater than (3,000) actually equaling (17,406), therefore it passes criteria checklist point (#9):

Sales ▾
9,688
2,507
1,449
1,293
1,085
314
306
249
151
142
83
76
63

Method #10: Determining That At Least (6) Out Of The Top (16) Competitors Generate A Total Monthly Sales Volume Of No Less Than (300) Units.

      For this task you will be individually evaluating each of the top (1-16) competitors total monthly unit sales volume. The reason for performing this procedure is to verify that the market you are attempting to enter has at least (6) out of the top (16) competitors retailing no less (300) units on a monthly basis. Ultimately, (300) monthly unit sales volume is a healthy amount of consumer purchases and should be one of your initial goals especially when first starting out as a new seller on Amazon entering a fresh market. I would not recommend entering a market where you cannot retail at least (10) units a day due to the fact that it can negatively impact your (FBA) storage fee rates, (IPI) Index Performance Score, and overall total (ROI).

      Effectively, if you retail (300) units a month as new seller you could start out with a small mass order of (900-1000) units from your supplier and intend on ordering more product on a (2) month or quarterly basis. You could then slowly increase your order amounts as you attempt to rank to the top of the specific subcategory you retail in exponentially growing your business from small to large. That topic will be comprehensively covered in detail in subsequent chapters, but for now I would simply like you to understand why (300) monthly unit sales volume with an inventory turnover rate of at least (4) times a year is a healthy initial goal to strive for.

      *As you can observe in the screenshot below, through utilization of Helium 10's Amazon product research tool Xray you can quickly and easily individually investigate the top (1-16) competitors' total monthly unit sales volume. Furthermore, upon examination of the provided data I have concluded that (7) out of the top (1-16) competitors have a monthly unit sales volume greater than (300), therefore it passes criteria checklist point (#10):

Sales ▾
9,688
2,507
1,449
1,293
1,085
314
306
249
151
142
83
76
63

Method #11: Determining That At Least (6) Out Of The Top (16) Competitors Generate A Yearly Total Sales Volume Of No Less Than (3600) Units.

For this task you will be individually navigating to each of the top (1-16) competitors and determining whether or not at least (6) of them are consistently retailing at least (300) units monthly over the course of a year totaling (3600) unit sales volume yearly. The reason for performing this procedure is to verify that this market is steady throughout the year and the product is not solely a seasonal item. If (6) out of the top (16) competitors product listings were only generating large amounts of sales at one or two times a year then the market you are researching is inconsistent and the product is most likely a seasonal item. I am not stating that retailing a seasonal item is necessarily a negative attribute for a product to have but it is something that you should take into account when you are researching products to sell due to the fact that it will impact how you structure your mass orders from your supplier, manage your product listing, stock your inventory, and run (PPC) Sponsored Ad Campaigns. Ultimately, if you are new to retailing products on the Amazon Marketplace I recommend opting to avoid selling seasonal merchandise until you first learn how to sell non-seasonal items. Ultimately, performing this process allows you to understand the market you are entering on a yearly basis so that you can plan for the future. If you intend on initially structuring your business on the (300) units a month sales volume by starting out with a small mass order of (900-1000) units from your supplier mentality as was discussed in Method #10 I would not recommend entering a seasonal market.

*Note: If you are intending on retailing seasonal merchandise you would alter Method #11 and would instead attempt to determine that at least (6) out of the top (16) competitors generate a sales volume of no less than (3600) units during the specific seasonal market you are focusing on entering.

To Determine That At Least (6) Out Of The Top (1-16) Competitors Generate A Yearly Total Sales Volume Of No Less Than (3600) Units, follow the instructional steps included with the labeled images below:

Step #1: Using your mouse, left-click and release on the top competitor's sales graph for "Baby Sling" from the Xray list created in a previous lesson to navigate to their sales chart:

Step #2: Using your mouse, left-click and release on the "1 Year" navigational task button:

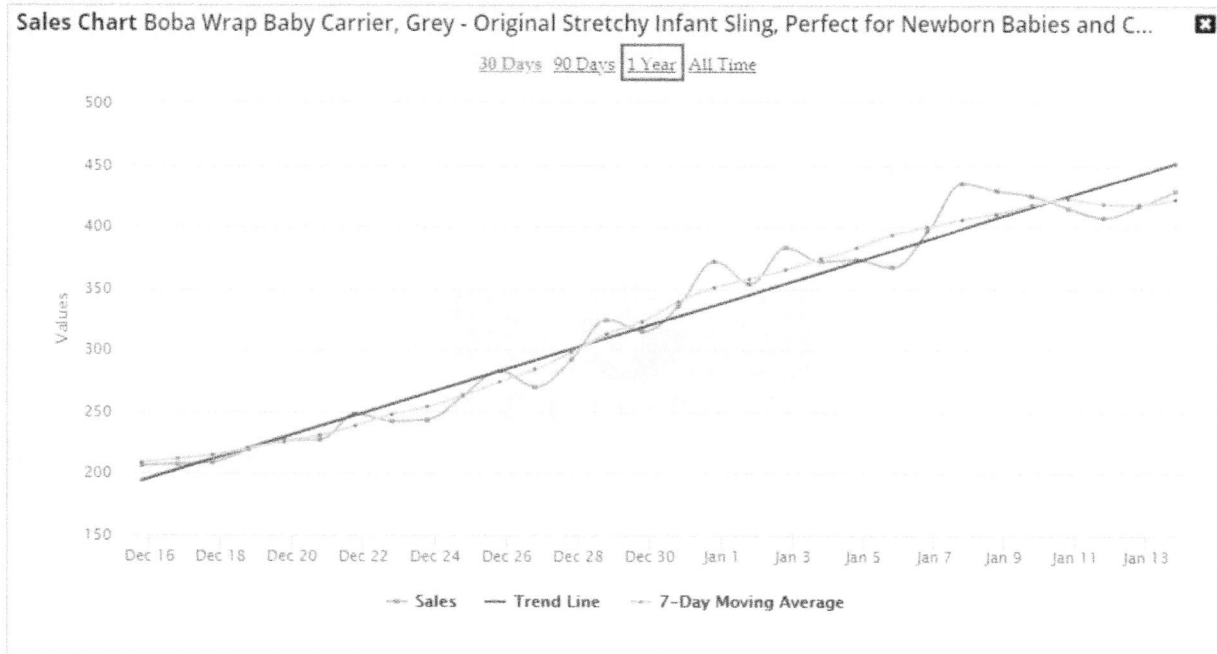

Sales Chart Boba Wrap Baby Carrier, Grey - Original Stretchy Infant Sling, Perfect for Newborn Babies and C...

Note: When you perform the task in Step #3 it is not necessary to get exact unit sales volume of each competitor's product listing you investigate as that would be painstakingly time consuming. You are merely attempting to get an approximated idea of whether or not at least (6) out of the top (1-16) competitors have at least (300) monthly unit sales and making certain that the market you are attempting to enter is not seasonal.

Step #3: Using your mouse, scroll over the entire year month by month and take note of the unit sales volume per month to determine whether the seller has a roughly estimated consistent sales of volume of at least (300) units per month throughout the year. Furthermore, if you notice that the product only retails large amounts for around (3) months out of the year and then drastically decreases to a very low amount or (0) unit sales volume for a (9) month period of time then this is an indication that the market for this product is seasonal:

Sales Chart Boba Wrap Baby Carrier, Grey - Original Stretchy Infant Sling, Perfect for Newborn Babies and C...

❖ Repeat this same task for the remainder of the top (1-16) competitors' product listings from the Xray list.

*Upon examination of each of the top (1-16) competitors' product listings yearly sales volume statistics I have concluded that (8) have a monthly unit sales volume of at least (300), therefore it passes criteria checklist point (#11).

Method #12: Determining That (1) Out Of The Top (16) Competitors Does Not Make Up More Than (75%) Of The Total Monthly Sales Volume.

For this task you will be making certain that one seller is not dominating the market you are attempting to enter. The reason for performing this procedure relies on the fact that if one seller is procuring (75%) or more of the total monthly sales volume they may either have a lot of external traffic, a hefty advertising budget, a patent on the product in question, or all of the above. If this is the case, then it will be difficult to dominate the market or play king of the hill so to speak with this seller. It will be next to impossible to dethrone them for the number one rank when the time comes to do so. Ultimately, you will be struggling to procure sales due to the fact that other sellers share is only (25%) of the monthly unit sales volume which means there is fierce competition among that small percentage. The best market to enter is one that has a somewhat equal distribution of sales volume among the top (1-16) competitors in any given keyword phrase or subcategory you are researching.

To Determine That (1) Out Of The Top (16) Competitors Does Not Make Up More Than (75%) Of The Total Monthly Sales Volume, follow the instructional steps included with the labeled images below:

Step #1: Add up the total sum of unit sales volume among the top (1-16) competitors' product listings sales data provided by Xray:

Sales ▾
9,688
2,507
1,449
1,293
1,085
314
306
249
151
142
83
76
63

- 9,688+2,507+1,449+1,293+1,085+314+306+249+151+142+83+76+63=17,406
- 75%=(17,406x.75=13,055)
- The top competitor of (1-16) has a total monthly sale volume of (9,688), which is less than (13,055) or (75%).

*Upon examination of the provided data I have concluded that one seller does not make up more than (75%) of the total sales volume for the keyword phrase "Baby Sling", therefore it passes criteria checklist point (#12).

Method #13: Determining That Less Than Half Of The Top (16) Competitors Are Recognizable Brand Names Or Well-Established Mainstream Companies.

If the market you are attempting to enter is dominated by recognizable brand names or well-established mainstream companies this means that they undoubtedly have the capability to acquire a lot of external traffic, have a hefty advertising budget, a patent on the product in question, or all of the above. What this means to you as an

Amazon Seller is that it will be extremely difficult to compete against them and next to impossible to dominate the market or play king of the hill so to speak. This is particularly true if the total number of sellers that make up more than half of the market share in a particular keyword phrase or subcategory you are researching are recognizable well-known brands. Ultimately, it will not be possible to dethrone these big brand name companies for the number one rank when the time comes to do so unless you pay big to play and have an extremely structured marketing campaign in place with an extensive advertising budget.

What I Mean By Recognizable Brand Names Or Well-Established Mainstream Companies:

For example, when researching the keyword phrase "Baby Sling" I am searching for big brand well-known baby retailers whose merchandise can be not only located online but also found in most brick & mortar stores, such as Target. For instance, I examined the top (1-16) competitors in search for baby brand names, such as:

- Johnson & Johnson
- Graco
- Fisher-Price
- Little Tikes
- Baby Einstein
- Ergobaby

*As you can observe in the screenshot below, through utilization of Helium 10's Amazon product research tool Xray you can quickly and easily individually investigate the top (1-16) competitors' brand names. Furthermore, upon examination of the provided data I have that (0) of the top (1-16) competitors retailing in this market are recognizable brand names or well-established mainstream companies, therefore it passes criteria checklist point (#13):

# ▲	ASIN	Brand	Title	Category
4	B005SP2LWW	Boba	Boba Wrap Baby Carrier, Grey - ...	Baby
5	B01AP8R6G2	Kangaroo...	Kangaroobaby Baby Sling Wrap ...	Baby
6	B071FDM61H	Nalakai	Luxury Ring Sling Baby Carrier - ...	Baby
7	B07QPYZMH4	Acrabros	Acrabros Baby Wrap Carrier,Ha...	Baby
8	B00OJVNSFA	Cuddlebug	9-in-1 CuddleBug Baby Wrap Sli...	Baby
9	B012ITT0RO	BabyWo...	Baby Wrap Carrier Ring Sling: Ex...	Baby
10	B01CYTYSR0	Sleepy W...	Baby Wrap Ergo Carrier Sling by...	Baby
11	B07MVVTPHP	Cuby	Baby Carrier by Cuby, Natural C...	Baby
12	B07NCNG75J	MEBIEN. ...	Baby Wrap Carrier Ring Sling-Lu...	Baby
13	B07SM127CR	5 STARS ...	Baby Wrap Carrier Sling Holder ...	Baby
14	B01B0SZOYM	Hip Baby ...	Hip Baby Wrap Ring Sling Baby ...	Baby
15	B07DKRXBB5	sweetbee	Lightweight My Honey Wrap - N...	Baby
16	B075SFW83N	Kids N' Su...	4 in 1 Baby Wrap Carrier and Ri...	Baby

Method #14: Determining That You Have The Ability To Differentiate The Product By Adding A Feature To It That Makes The Merchandise More Functional For The Consumer Or Provides A Sense Of Perceived Value In Contrast To The Top (16) Competitors.

As was discussed at the beginning of this chapter you can opt to reinvent/redesign an already existing product by differentiating it. You can manufacture a higher quality better developed option for customers to purchase than that of what your competitors are currently retailing on Amazon. With that stated, there are techniques you can utilize to discover what consumers like, dislike, or require as an added feature for a specific product you are researching.

To Learn What You Can Differentiate About A Product In Regard To Consumers Requests, follow the instructional steps included with the labeled images below:

Some sellers utilize black hat techniques that strictly violate Amazon (TOS), such as review manipulation or acquiring incentivized reviews. These reviews cannot be trusted for your statistical data analysis purposes as they are typically not authentic honest reviews that will paint a clear picture of what the consumer truly likes, dislikes, or requires in regard to differentiation in a product. Therefore, when you are examining reviews for a particular product listing I highly recommend utilizing the website www.fakespot.com which will help you determine whether or not the specific sellers reviews that you are researching are primarily real or fake.

How Fakespot's (A-F) Rating Values Operate:

- **A:** Excellent-All reviews are authentic.
- **B:** Good-All reviews are primarily authentic.
- **C:** Fair-All reviews are typically authentic but try to locate a review rating value of either (A) or (B) before settling for a (C).
- **D:** Not recommended as most reviews are primarily inauthentic.
- **F:** Highly unrecommended as all reviews are inauthentic.

Step #1: Using your mouse, left-click and release on the top competitor's (ASIN) for "Baby Sling" from the Xray list created in a previous lesson to navigate to the product listing detail page:

# ▲	ASIN	Brand	Title	Category
4	B005SP2LWW	Boba	Boba Wrap Baby Carrier, Grey - ...	Baby
5	B01AP8R6G2	Kangaroo...	Kangaroobaby Baby Sling Wrap ...	Baby
6	B071FDM61H	Nalakai	Luxury Ring Sling Baby Carrier – ...	Baby
7	B07QPYZMH4	Acrabros	Acrabros Baby Wrap Carrier,Ha...	Baby
8	B00OJVNSFA	Cuddlebug	9-in-1 CuddleBug Baby Wrap Sli...	Baby
9	B012iTT0RO	BabyWo...	Baby Wrap Carrier Ring Sling: Ex...	Baby
10	B01CYTYSR0	Sleepy W...	Baby Wrap Ergo Carrier Sling by...	Baby
11	B07MVVTPHP	Cuby	Baby Carrier by Cuby, Natural C...	Baby
12	B07NCNG75J	MEBIEN. ...	Baby Wrap Carrier Ring Sling-Lu...	Baby
13	B07SM127CR	5 STARS ...	Baby Wrap Carrier Sling Holder ...	Baby
14	B01B0SZOYM	Hip Baby ...	Hip Baby Wrap Ring Sling Baby ...	Baby
15	B07DKRXBB5	sweetbee	Lightweight My Honey Wrap - N...	Baby
16	B075SFW83N	Kids N' Su...	4 in 1 Baby Wrap Carrier and Ri...	Baby

Step #2: Copy the product listings direct Amazon (URL) located in your Google Chrome Web Browser search bar:

ⓘ amazon.com/dp/B005SP2LWW

Step #3: Navigate to www.fakespot.com from within the Google Chrome Web Browser.

Step #4: Paste the product listings direct Amazon (URL) into into Fakespots generator:

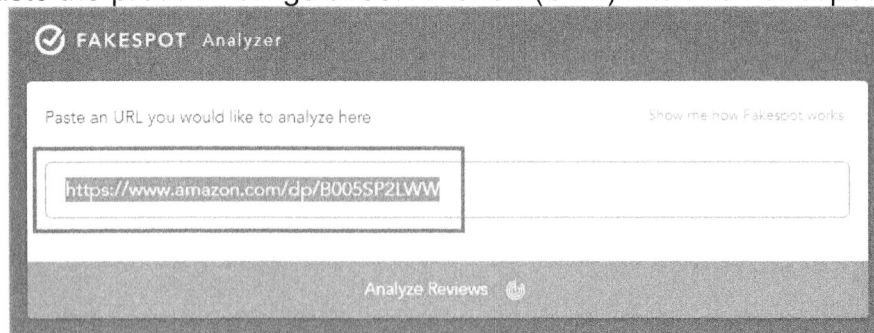

◉ FAKESPOT Analyzer

Paste an URL you would like to analyze here   Show me how Fakespot works

https://www.amazon.com/dp/B005SP2LWW

Analyze Reviews

Step #5: Using your mouse, left-click and release on the "Analyze Reviews" navigational task button:

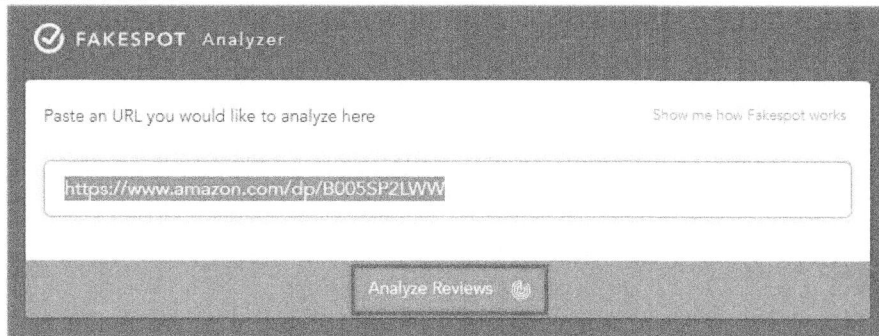

Step #6: Look for the product listing review score located on the top right-hand side of the page:

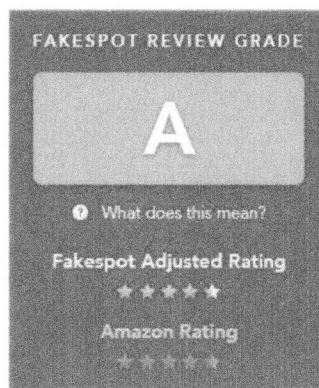

❖ As you can observe, this product listing scored an (A) which is an excellent rating therefore I will utilize it for statistical data review analysis.

Step #7: Now that you have verified that this seller's reviews are authentic you will navigate back to your top competitor's Amazon product listing detail page for the (ASIN) B005SP2LWW. From the seller's product listing detail page you will use your mouse to left-click and release on Helium 10's Google Chrome Extension located on the top right-hand side of the Google Chrome Web Browser which will generate a list of navigational task buttons:

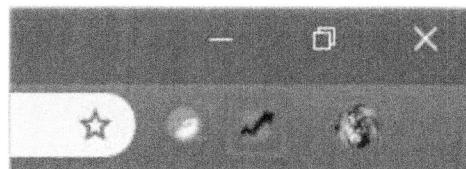

Step #8: Using your mouse, left-click and release on Helium 10's Amazon product research tool "Review Downloader" to generate a list of options:

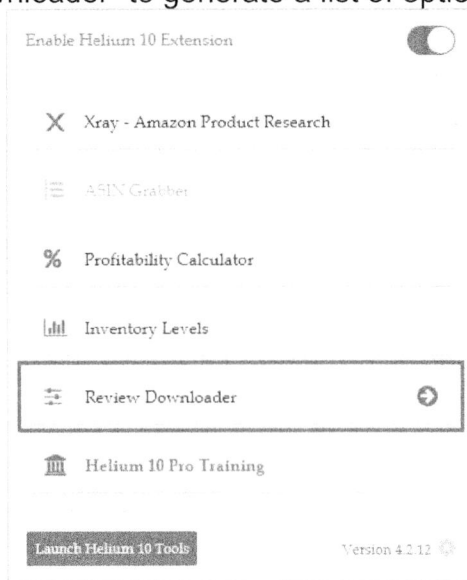

Step #9: Be certain to:

- Turn on "Only Verified Purchase"
- Turn the (4-5) star ratings off

    Using your mouse, left-click and release on the "Extract" navigational task button:

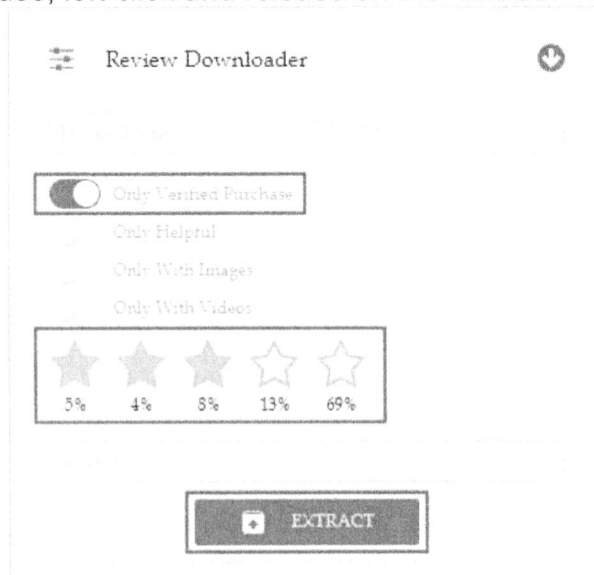

Step #10: Read through the reviews.

    To read through the reviews manually utilize the "All Reviews" section:

OR:

To read through the reviews by identifying specific keywords and keyword phrases utilize the "Analysis" tab located at the top of the page:

ANALYSIS

*Upon examination of the provided data from Helium 10's Review Downloader I located (3) possible added features that are being requested by the consumer that could differentiate my product from that of my competitors:

1) Several consumers review comments have requested that the baby sling have a small pocket for carrying keys or a cellphone added to the material on the front of the product. I could opt to discuss this feature with a supplier and have the pocket added to the product when it is manufactured.

2) Several consumers review comments have noted that the fabric is too thick and hot to wear, especially in the summer months, therefore I could opt to have the product manufactured with thinner less dense fabric that allows the skin to breathe thus alleviating this issue.

3) Several consumers review comments have discussed the fact that the product does not come with clear concise directions on proper use. Therefore, they have requested that there be a short DVD/Blu-ray video or a link to one that illustrates how to properly attach the garment and carry their baby while using the sling. I could opt to write clearer directions on using the product as well create a short YouTube video which could be offered as a direct link in the instructional booklet.

   ❖ With the (3) added features product identified I have determined that this product can be differentiated, therefore it passes criteria checklist point (#14).

Pro Tip:

When you are examining your top competitors' reviews do not solely look for features you can add to your product to make it more functional but also focus on the positive remark's consumers are expressing as well as the negative. You can then utilize these comments to learn what customers either like or dislike about a particular product. You can then opt to add the positive elements they love about the product to your merchandise when it is manufactured if it does not already have the specific aspect and you can also alter or remove the negative qualities they dislike about the product if your merchandise has similar features.

*Note: If you are intending on reading negative reviews set the star rating to only (1-3) star reviews when you utilize Helium 10's review downloader which will solely download & include the low-star reviews for you to evaluate. On the contrary, if you are intending on reading positive reviews change the star rating to only (4-5) star reviews when you utilize Helium 10's review downloader which will solely download and include the high-star reviews for you to evaluate.

Furthermore, you can also utilize reviews to locate which variation of a product retails the most units. This information can be highly beneficial if you are unsure which color or dimensions of a product to manufacture and sell. Ultimately, you should utilize the data provided by Helium 10 in regard to variations to make executive business decisions. What I do not recommend is basing your decisions on a guess or your own opinion. What I mean by this statement, is do not source and retail a product solely centered on the fact that you may prefer one particular color or dimension over another because customers may have an entirely different view.

To Learn What Variation Of A Product Retails The Most Units, follow the instructional steps included with the labeled images below:

Step #1: Using your mouse, left-click and release on the top competitor's (ASIN) for "Baby Sling" from the Xray list created in a previous lesson to navigate to the product listing detail page:

# ▲	ASIN	Brand	Title	Category
4	B005SP2LWW	Boba	Boba Wrap Baby Carrier, Grey - ...	Baby
5	B01AP8R6G2	Kangaroo...	Kangaroobaby Baby Sling Wrap ...	Baby
6	B071FDM61H	Nalakai	Luxury Ring Sling Baby Carrier – ...	Baby
7	B07QPYZMH4	Acrabros	Acrabros Baby Wrap Carrier,Ha...	Baby
8	B000JVNSFA	Cuddlebug	9-in-1 CuddleBug Baby Wrap Sli...	Baby
9	B012ITT0RO	BabyWo...	Baby Wrap Carrier Ring Sling: Ex...	Baby
10	B01CYTYSR0	Sleepy W...	Baby Wrap Ergo Carrier Sling by...	Baby
11	B07MVVTPHP	Cuby	Baby Carrier by Cuby, Natural C...	Baby
12	B07NCNG75J	MEBIEN. ...	Baby Wrap Carrier Ring Sling-Lu...	Baby
13	B07SM127CR	5 STARS ...	Baby Wrap Carrier Sling Holder ...	Baby
14	B01B0SZOYM	Hip Baby ...	Hip Baby Wrap Ring Sling Baby ...	Baby
15	B07DKRXBB5	sweetbee	Lightweight My Honey Wrap - N...	Baby
16	B075SFW83N	Kids N' Su...	4 in 1 Baby Wrap Carrier and Ri...	Baby

*Note: Although I am not illustrating utilization of www.fakespot for this lesson be certain to always check if the reviews are authentic before moving forward to the following step as was learned in the previous exercise.

Step #2: From the seller's product listing detail page you will use your mouse to left-click and release on Helium 10's Google Chrome Extension located on the top right-hand side of the Google Chrome Web Browser which will generate a list of navigational task buttons:

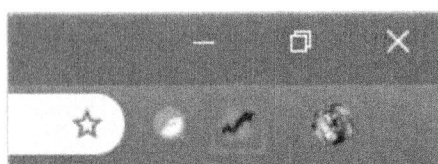

Step #3: Using your mouse, left-click and release on Helium 10's Amazon product research tool "Review Downloader" to generate a list of options:

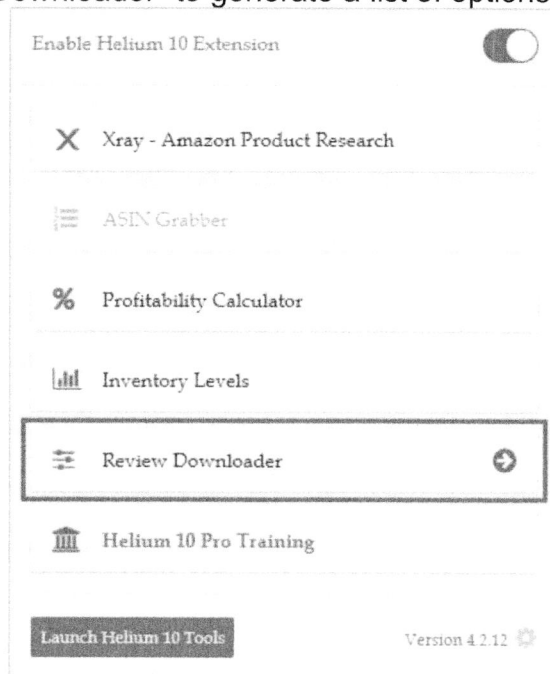

Enable Helium 10 Extension

X Xray - Amazon Product Research

ASIN Grabber

% Profitability Calculator

Inventory Levels

Review Downloader

Helium 10 Pro Training

Launch Helium 10 Tools   Version 4.2.12

Step #4: Be certain to:

- Turn on "Only Verified Purchase"
- Leave all (5) stars turned on

Using your mouse, left-click and release on the "Extract" navigational task button:

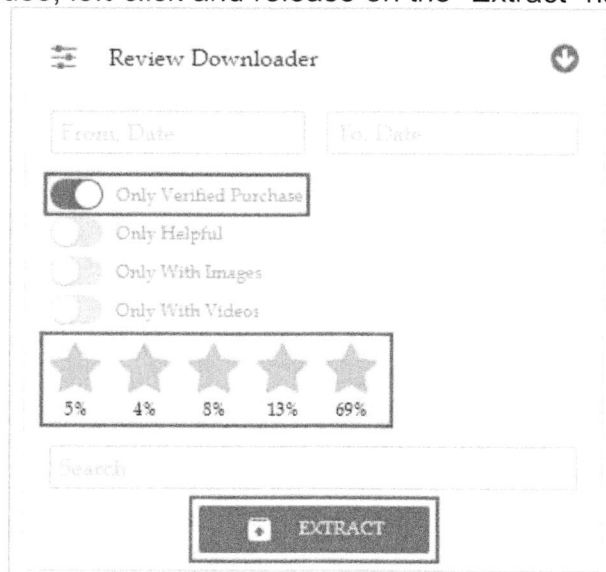

Review Downloader

From Date   To Date

Only Verified Purchase
Only Helpful
Only With Images
Only With Videos

5%   4%   8%   13%   69%

Search

EXTRACT

Step #5: As you can observe in the screenshot below, the list that appears at the top of the page of the "All Reviews" section contains the entire batch of variations this particular seller retails of this specific product. As you can observe in the screenshot below, as you examine the list of product variations you will identify the (ASIN) with the highest review count which is an indication that this variation retails the most units in contrast to the other variations of the product. With that stated, if I was truly attempting to retail a similar product to that of this sellers I would definitely initially source the color variation or something similar to that associated with the (ASIN) B005SP2LWW due to the fact that the data has identified that this is the most popular color variation amongst the other available options. Ultimately, customers prefer this specific variation in contrast to the others. I am not stating that this should be the only variation of a product you should retail but it is definitely an initial starting point. You could then work your way up to carrying several more variations of the product as you grow your brand.

Boba Wrap Baby Carrier, Grey - Original Stretchy Infant Sling, Perfect for Newborn Babies and Children up to 35 lbs

Average rating 4.4

ASIN	Style	Review Count	Review Share	Average Rating
B005SP5TX0	Format: Baby Product	510	19%	4.1
B005SP2LWW	Format: Baby Product	1549	57%	4.2
B073VQWF7Q	Format: Baby Product	10	0%	4.5
B0161B76XK	Format: Baby Product	45	2%	4.3
B00NMOE2ZK	Format: Baby Product	178	7%	4.3
B071KC4QYG	Format: Electronics	4	0%	5
B071GR5115	Format: Baby Product	3	0%	5
B005SOP4EA	Format: Baby Product	120	4%	4.1
B001CWHK44	Format: Baby Product	98	4%	4.3
B076H2S2LD	Format: Baby Product	7	0%	5
B07GZPQ9S2	Format: Baby Product	6	0%	4.7
B0774X9RZD	Format: Baby Product	11	0%	4.2
B0161BBMGC	Format: Baby Product	24	1%	4.4
B072J9LPXY	Format: Baby Product	5	0%	5
B07R4W7MSG	Format: Baby Product	1	0%	5
B01N5SCO9I	Format: Baby Product	3	0%	5
B074N28TQV	Format: Baby Product	1	0%	5

Method #15: Determining That The Top (16) Competitors Have Noticeable Differences In Their Product Listing Price Points.

For this task you will be making certain that among the top (1-16) competitors there is noticeable product listing price point differences. A clear variation in sellers' prices allows room for you to either retail your merchandise at a higher price point due to it being a better quality product with added features or price it a bit lower to compete with some of the top seller's offers. If all the sellers are retailing their merchandise at the same exact price point and you price yours higher then you may find that you will be unsuccessful in the market you entered. If all products are priced differently the consumer will tend to look through the offers a bit more carefully because some may be better than others. On the contrary, if all the products are priced equally, depending on the merchandise in question, the consumer will spend less time looking through the offers and generally just purchase from the very top of the list. What I mean by this, is that if the prices are all similar there is no room for differentiation and to procure sales you would typically be forced to price your product the same or lower just to compete with the other sellers. Furthermore, if all the top sellers in a particular market have their products priced identically eventually they will typically all begin to compete solely on price points which means over time the cost of the product may get lower and lower until it hits rock bottom.

*As you can observe in the screenshot below, through utilization of Helium 10's Amazon product research tool Xray you can quickly and easily individually investigate the top (1-16) competitors' product listing price points. Furthermore, upon examination of the provided data I have concluded that there are noticeable differences in each competitor's price points, therefore it passes criteria checklist point (#15):

Price ▾
$59.90
$49.95
$49.95
$39.95
$39.95
$29.99
$29.99
$29.07
$22.92
$21.99
$19.99
$17.95
$13.69

Method #16: Determining That You Have The Ability To Retail The Product For No Less Than (5x) The Landing Costs.

To compete for sales on Amazon you will most likely be pricing your merchandise similarly to that of other sellers, therefore the first step in determining the your ability to retail your product for (5x) the landing costs is to investigate your top competitor's product price point, which will give you a general approximated idea of what you can sell a comparable type of merchandise for on Amazon.

*As you can observe in the screenshot below, through utilization of Helium 10's Amazon product research tool Xray you can quickly and easily individually investigate the top competitor's product price point. Furthermore, from this data I have gathered that to successfully compete with the top competitor on Amazon you would most likely have to keep your product priced somewhere roughly within the ($39.95-$44.95) range, depending on the added features you opt for when manufacturing:

# ▲	ASIN	Brand	Title	Category	BuyBox	#	🚚	Price
5	B005SP2LWW	Boba	Boba Wrap Baby Carrier, Grey - ...	Baby	Boba Inc. (USA)	1	FBA	$39.95

To determine your product cost you would then navigate to www.alibaba.com and perform a search for "Baby Sling" where you would locate either the same merchandise or something similar to get an approximated cost per unit. As you can observe in the screenshot below, the estimated manufacturing cost per unit for the exact same baby sling that currently retails on Amazon is ($2.37-2.58). Please be aware, this per unit cost is never typically the actual price you will pay, which will be discussed in much greater detail in Chapter 9. For now, I merely want you to understand how to configure an estimated product manufacturing cost when you are conducting statistical data analysis. A good rule of thumb is to always go with the higher cost when estimating this calculation:

Amazon newest trending best sale ergonomic lightweight organic cotton

$2.37-$2.58 / Piece

4 Pieces (Min Order)

5 buyers

Gaoyang Hongchang Towel Factory

CN 11 YRS

65.6% 4.3 ★ 10 reviews | "Quick servi...

The next step is to determine your total landing costs. Although, Helium 10's profitability calculator can give you a brief summarized rough estimate of landing costs, when you are conducting product discovery I recommend manually configuring each expense from the following list in contrast to basing your calculations solely on their tool alone. For the purposes of this lesson, I have spoken to one of my suppliers in regard to the manufacturing expenses associated with a baby sling so that I can offer you a true example of landing costs.

When Determining A Products Landing Costs Several Production Expenses Must Be Considered, Such As:

- Manufacturing
- Branding (Optional)
- Brand Trademark Fees (Optional)
- Individual Product Packaging
- (FNSKU) Labels
- Shipping From Your Supplier To Your Location Or The Amazon Fulfillment Center
- Third Party Inspection Service
- Shipping To The Amazon Fulfillment Center If You Choose To Intercept & Personally Inspect The Merchandise (FBA Only)

Baby Sling Total Landing Cost:

Manufacturing=($3.35/Unit With Added Features=Pocket, Lighter Fabric)

Branding=($.20/Unit=Small Brand Logo Printed On Fabric Of The Product)

Individual Product Packaging=($.49/Unit=Bubble Wrap Mailer)

Branding=($.05/Unit=Sticker With Brand Logo For Placement On Bubble Wrap Mailer) (FNSKU) Labels=(.02/Unit)

Shipping= From Supplier Directly To The Amazon Fulfillment Center (SEA)-Door To Door Express=($1.09/Unit)

Total Per Unit Manufacturing Costs Before Additional Expenses Added:

- 3.35+.20+.49+.05+.02+$1.09=$5.20

Additional Expenses:

Brand Trademark Fees=($225)

(UPC)=($40/UPC=GS1)

Third Party Inspection Service=($188 Flat Rate Fee=China Certification & Inspection Group)

Additional Expenses Divided By Mass Order Amount:

- $225/1000 Units=($.23/Unit)
- $40/1000 Units=($.04/Unit)
- $188/1000 Units=($.19/Unit)

Total Per Unit Manufacturing Costs After Additional Expenses Added:

- 3.35+.20+.49+.05+.02+$1.09+.23+.04+.19=($5.66/Unit)

Baby Sling Product Price Point On Amazon & Conclusion:

With the added features I would initially retail this product for ($44.95) which means that at a total per unit manufacturing cost of ($5.66/Unit) it would retail for (8x) the landing cost; therefore it passes criteria checklist point (#16).

Method #17: Determining That You Have The Ability To Generate A Gross Profitability Margin Of No Less Than (30%).

The final step in statistical data analysis is to determine your total estimated gross profitability margin. Although, Helium 10's profitability calculator can give you a brief summarized rough estimate of profitability margins, when you are conducting product discovery I recommend manually configuring each expense from the list below in contrast to basing your calculations solely on their tool alone. For the purposes of this lesson, I have utilized the (FBA) fee schedules from Chapter 2.

When Determining A Products Estimated Gross Profitability Margin Several Production Costs Must Be Considered, Such As:

- Manufacturing
- Branding (Optional)
- Brand Trademark Fees (Optional)
- Individual Packaging
- (UPC)
- (FNSKU) Labels
- Third Party Inspection Service
- Shipping From Your Supplier To Your Location
- Shipping To The Amazon Fulfillment Center (FBA Only)
- (FBA) Fees (Storage, Pick, Pack, & Shipping) (FBA Only)
- Amazon Referral Fees
- Shipping To The Customer (MFN Only)
- Advertising (Amazon Sponsored Ad Campaigns: Automatic & Manual)
- Amazon's (ERP) Early Reviewer Program: ($60)

Approx $1 per unit (handwritten annotation)

- ❖ To receive an estimated per unit gross profitability margin, you would take the retail cost you intend on selling your product for and deduct the total sum of production costs.

To Determine A Products Per Unit Gross Profitability Margin:

- Product Price Point-Production Costs=Gross Profit

Baby Sling Total Estimated Production Cost:

Landing Costs=($5.66/Unit)

- (1000 Units x $5.66=$5,660)

(FBA) Fees=($5.24/Unit)

- (1000 Units x $5.24=$5,240)

Amazon Referral Fees=($44.95x0.15=$6.74/Unit)

- (1000 Units x $6.74=$6,740)

Advertising=20%=(1000 Units x 0.20=$200)

- Per Unit Advertising Cost Of Sale=(200/1000 Units=$0.20/Unit)

- Total Advertising Cost Of Sale=($200)

Amazon's (ERP)=($60)

Production Costs Per Unit:

- 5.66+5.24+6.74+0.20=($17.84)

Total Product Costs For (1000) Units:

- 5,660+5,240+6,740+200+60=($17,900)

Baby Sling Estimated Per Unit Gross Profitability Margin:

- $44.95-$17.84=($27.11)

30% Of $44.95 Is:

$44.95x0.30=$13.49

*The estimated per unit profit made off of retailing a baby sling is=($27.11) which is well over the ($13.49 or 30%) profitability margin needed, therefore it passes criteria checklist point (#17).

❖ After conducting statistical data analysis utilizing the criteria checklist the "Baby Sling" product has scored a (16/17) which means that this merchandise is definitely a viable profitable option to source and retail on the Amazon Marketplace.

*Cautionary Note: Although, the "Baby Sling" did score (16/17), which makes it a viable profitable product to retail, this product evaluation example is merely for educational purposes. Furthermore, numerous individuals are reading this material so by no means am I recommending that you opt for this exact type of merchandise as your option to retail on the Amazon Marketplace.

Pro Tip #1:

Once you choose a viable profitable product to retail on Amazon, before you have your merchandise manufactured, I recommend ordering (1) product unit from (1-2) of the top sellers within the specific market you are entering as well as heavily investigating their Amazon product listings. By performing these tasks, you can look for attributes to optimize when you have a similar product manufactured and build your product listings that will create an enhanced experience for your customers.

Competitor Product Attributes Research Checklist:

o   What condition did the product arrive in? Did it have scratches, broken, or missing pieces?
o   Would the product be better with an added feature or two?
o   Does the product come with a case for carrying and storage?
o   How did the product come packaged upon receival and would you change anything about its packaging?
o   Was the product unboxing experience pleasant?
o   Is the product made out of strong durable high-quality materials or could they be altered and improved?
o   Does the product come with instructions on how to use and care for the merchandise? If not, you may want to add this to your product as an insert in the product packaging or printed directly on the product packaging.
o   Is there a product insert in the packaging asking you to leave a review and star rating on the seller's product listing for the specific product you purchased? If, so how is the insert worded and what is the insert printed on?
o   Does the product price point seem fair from a consumer's point of view? Ultimately, is the expense incurred worth the merchandise? If not, you may want to price your product a bit lower to make the purchase more cost worthy for the customer.
o   Does the product come with an added surprise gift, such as a promotional item or a small additional product that was undisclosed in the product listing?
o   Did you receive a follow-up email from the seller thanking you for your purchase?
o   Overall, what are the positive attributes about the product? What would you replicate?

o   Overall, what are the negative attributes about the product? What would you change and optimize?

Competitor Product Listing Attributes Research Checklist:

o   Is the product title, bullet points, and description accurately written in comparison to the product you received?
o   Is the product title, bullet points, and description too long?
o   Is the product title, bullet points, and description confusing?
o   Is the product title, bullet points, and description well-written?
o   What keywords and keyword phrases do they utilize in their product title, bullet points, and description?
o   Is the product information accurate?
o   What questions have customers asked about the product in the Q&A section of the product listing?
o   What do the customers product reviews reveal?
o   Are the customer reviews primarily positive or negative?
o   Are the product images high-quality & professional grade?
o   Are there lifestyle images of the product showing it in use?
o   Is there a total of (9) images?
o   Are the product features well showcased in the product images?
o   Is there a video of the product being used?
o   Do they offer variations of the product?
o   Is the product (FBA) or (MFN)?
o   Overall, what are the positive attributes about the product listing? What would you replicate?
o   Overall, what are the negative attributes about the product listing? What would you change and optimize?

Pro Tip #2:

When you are first choosing a product to retail as an Amazon Seller new to the business I recommend dividing your total initial investment by (2.5) and only spending that amount on your first mass order product landing costs. The rest of the money will be reserved for product launch, (PPC) Sponsored Ad Marketing Campaigns, and most importantly your next order of products. Being prepared for your next order ahead of time is crucial to successfully building a business as an Amazon Seller. Ultimately, the day your first order makes it to the Amazon Fulfillment Center you should be placing your next order of the same exact merchandise from your supplier to avoid a stock-out scenario due to the fact that each time you run out of stock you will typically lose rank on Amazon. The longer you are out of stock the further you will fall in rank therefore if you are in search of longevity for your business be certain to plan ahead by saving a portion of your initial investment for a reorder.

Example:

Initial Investment Amount: ($6,000)

($6,000/2.5)=($2,400)

This means that you only have a maximum of ($2,400) for your first mass order of merchandise. The rest of your cashflow should be utilized for marketing and your next order of product to replenish your inventory on Amazon.

*Understanding how to properly utilize product discovery to choose viable profitable merchandise to retail on the Amazon Marketplace is a significant essential milestone in remaining a successful Amazon Seller.

Conclusion:

I truly hope that "Amazon Seller Classroom In A Book: Methods Of Product Research" has exceeded your expectations, that you found it informative, and that the lessons within significantly accommodate you in your Amazon focused e-commerce ventures. Now that you formally understand the entire process from (A-Z) of how to effectively conduct product discovery to locate viable lucrative merchandise to retail on the Amazon Marketplace I recommend purchasing the "The Official Amazon Seller Classroom In A Book: Volume II" and continuing your educational experience.

*If you could please kindly take a moment to leave an honest review and star rating on Amazon for your purchase of my book that would be greatly appreciated.

The Official Amazon Seller Classroom In A Book: VOLUME II Includes:

- **(1)** In-Depth Chapter That Contains Over **(20)** Step-By-Step Walk-Through Tutorials With Accompanying Images That You Can Follow Along With On Your Computer As You Work Your Way Through Volume II That Will Teach You The Entire Process From (A-Z) Of How To Effectively Source High-Quality Merchandise From Reputable (B2B) Marketplace Suppliers Online & Build Identifiable Sophisticated Brands.

- **(4)** Detailed Email Templates Containing Commonly Asked Questions That You Can Utilize When You Correspond With Product Manufacturers & You Are Sourcing Merchandise From Suppliers.

In "The Official Amazon Seller Classroom In A Book: Volume II" you will learn how to:

- ✓ Build Identifiable Sophisticated Brands

- ✓ Design Your Primary Company Name, Brand Names, & Brand Logos Utilizing Vector Graphic Software

- ✓ Create A Professional "Business Identity Verified" Alibaba Marketplace Account

- ✓ Locate & Source Exceptional Merchandise From Reputable Suppliers On (B2B) Marketplace Platforms

- ✓ Choose Individual Product Packaging For Your Merchandise & Get It Branded With Your Primary Company Name, Brand Name, & Brand Logos

- ✓ Private Label Products With Your Unique Company Name, Brand Names, & Brand Logos

- ✓ Obtain (UPCs) & (FNSKUs) For Your Merchandise

✓ Handle (SEA) & (AIR) Freight Mass Order Shipments; Each Type Outlined: How, What, When, & Why Explained

✓ Properly Prepare, Package, & Ship Mass Orders Of Merchandise To The Amazon Fulfilment Center When Utilizing The (FBA) Program

*Note: If you do not already own a copy of **Volume II** and would like to continue your learning experience please refer to the provided link below:

http://amazon.com/dp/B07ZXL74WZ

Exclusive Facebook Group For Amazon Sellers:

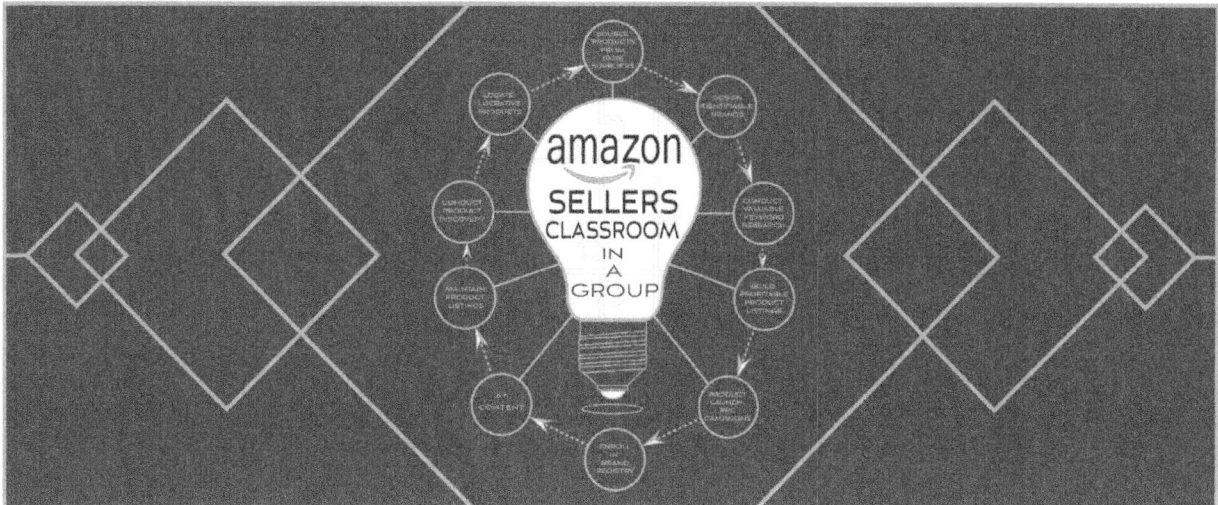

Amazon Sellers Classroom In A Group | FBA & FBM Mastery is an exclusive Facebook focus group designed specifically for all levels of Amazon Sellers to network with one another in a united community setting and get answers to questions related to retailing merchandise on the Amazon Marketplace via FBA & FBM. Furthermore, it is place where informative Amazon Seller updates, secrets, tips, strategies, & ideas are shared on a weekly basis by the author of this book Drew Berry as well as other specific top sellers in the e-commerce industry.

Members Of The Group Have Access To:

- Watch Parties Where Specific Top Seller Strategies Are Revealed
- Monthly Drawings & Giveaways To Select Content
- Amazon Seller Webinars
- Amazon Seller Classes
- Amazon Seller Consulting

To Join The Group Free Of Charge Please Refer To The Provided Link Below:

www.facebook.com/groups/amzsellers/

FREE GIFT: One-On-One (5) Question Live Email Correspondence With The Author:

If you require additional instructional assistance in regard to the information in this book, necessitate further guidance on any aspect of being an Amazon Seller, or have general inquiries about properly conducting product discovery be sure to personally email me your list of questions at the address provided below.

Eligibility Requirements, Criteria, Policies, & Email Address:

PROOF OF PURCHASE:

- In Order To Receive The Free Gift, Purchase Of "Amazon Seller Classroom In A Book: Methods Of Product Research" Is Required
- Date Of Purchase
- Purchase Order #
- A Screenshot Of The Transaction Receipt/Invoice For Your Purchase Of This Book From Kindle Is Required & Must Be Sent With The Initial Email Containing Your Questions To Verify Your Order.

Criteria:

- (5) Question Maximum Limit Per Proof Of Purchase
- Questions Must be Received In An Organized Numbered (1-5) List Format

Policy:

- (1) Redemption Per Verified Proof Of Purchase

Email Questions To The Provided Address Below:

- officialamzseller@gmail.com

Printed in Great Britain
by Amazon